Veronika Bernard

Images of the City

ETHNOLOGIE

ANTHROPOLOGY

Band / Volume 56

LIT

Veronika Bernard

IMAGES OF THE CITY

LIT

For Serhan

Cover photos © Veronika Bernard

Photos (top left to bottom right/ oben links – unten rechts):
Visual Deception no. 2 (Istanbul, 2013)
Illuminated Istanbul (Istanbul, 2013)
Steel Flowers (Lyon, 2011)
It's a Bright Life no. 2 (Bratislava, 2013)

Bibliographic information published by the Deutsche Nationalbibliothek
The Deutsche Nationalbibliothek lists this publication in the Deutsche Nationalbibliografie; detailed bibliographic data are available in the Internet at http://dnb.d-nb.de.

ISBN 978-3-643-50594-1

A catalogue record for this book is available from the British Library

Klosbachstr. 107
CH-8032 Zürich
Tel. +41 (0) 44-251 75 05
Fax +41 (0) 44-251 75 06
E-Mail: zuerich@lit-verlag.ch
http://www.lit-verlag.ch

LIT VERLAG Dr. W. Hopf
Berlin 2014
Fresnostr. 2
D-48159 Münster
Tel. +49 (0) 2 51-62 03 20
Fax +49 (0) 2 51-23 19 72
E-Mail: lit@lit-verlag.de
http://www.lit-verlag.de

Distribution:

In the UK: Global Book Marketing, e-mail: mo@centralbooks.com
In North America: International Specialized Book Services, e-mail: orders@isbs.com
In Germany: LIT Verlag Fresnostr. 2, D-48159 Münster
Tel. +49 (0) 2 51-620 32 22, Fax +49 (0) 2 51-922 60 99, E-mail: vertrieb@lit-verlag.de

In Austria: Medienlogistik Pichler-ÖBZ, e-mail: mlo@medien-logistik.at
e-books are available at www.litwebshop.de

Table of Contents - Inhaltsverzeichnis

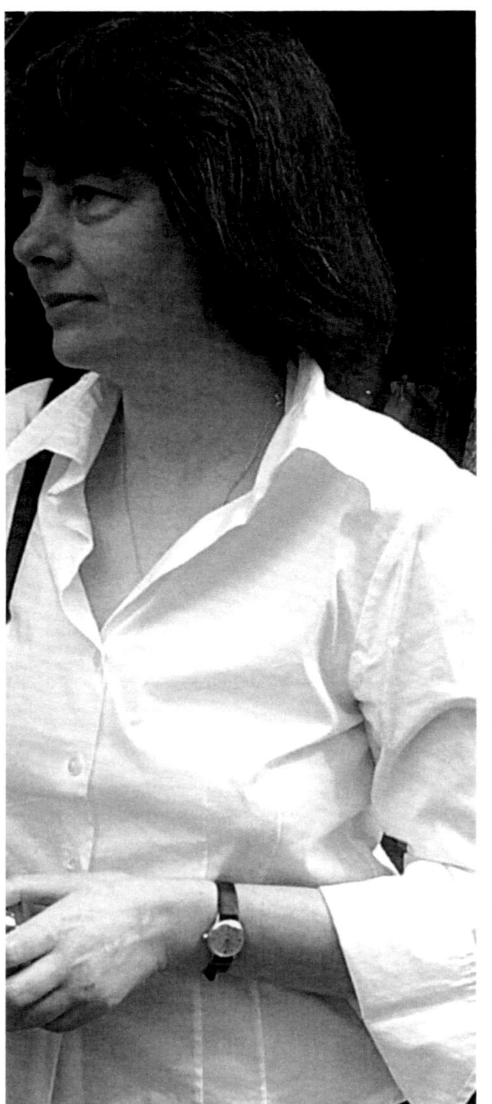

Photo © by Serhan Oksay (2009)

Images of the City

IMAGES OF THE CITY is a photographic album devoted to urban culture. The 50 photos were taken at several European cities in the years 2007 – 2013 as part of my digital arts projects *ORNAMENTAL ABSTRACTIONS* and *SNAPSHOTS* and also as part of my academic projects *BREAKING THE STEREOTYPE* and *IMAGES*, the latter of which I developed together with Serhan Oksay in 2010.
The photos understand urban culture as the process and result of the creative and technological adaptation of nature and as a life style.

IMAGES OF THE CITY ist ein der Kultur des urbanen Raumes gewidmeter Bildband. Er vereint eine Auswahl von 50 Fotos, die ich in den Jahren 2007 – 2013 im Rahmen meiner beiden Kunst- und Fotografie-Projekte *ORNAMENTAL ABSTRACTIONS* und *SNAPSHOTS* in europäischen Städten aufgenommen habe. Einige der Fotos entstanden als Teil meiner akademischen Projekte *BREAKING THE STEREOTYPE* und *IMAGES - Bilder, die man sich macht*, deren letzteres ich gemeinsam mit Serhan Oksay im Jahr 2010 entwickelte.
Die Fotos interpretieren Kultur des urbanen Raumes als die von Menschen kreativ, technisch und industriell gestaltete Landschaft und als den daraus resultierenden Lebensstil.

Veronika Bernard

Arranged Nature

Gestaltete Natur

IMAGES OF THE CITY

Photo no. 1: "Artificial Cave"

by Veronika Bernard

Avignon, 2011

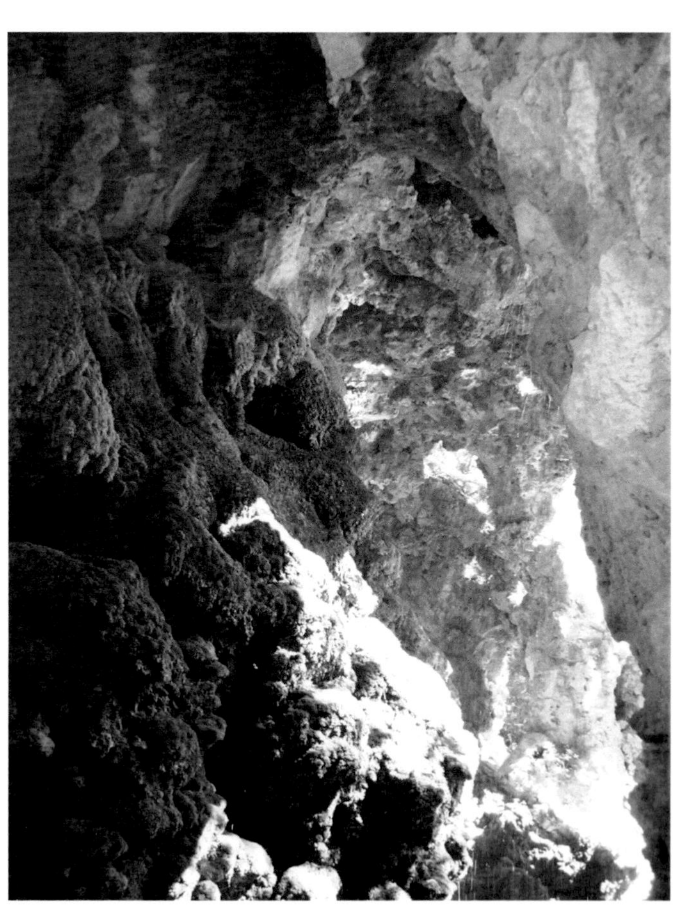

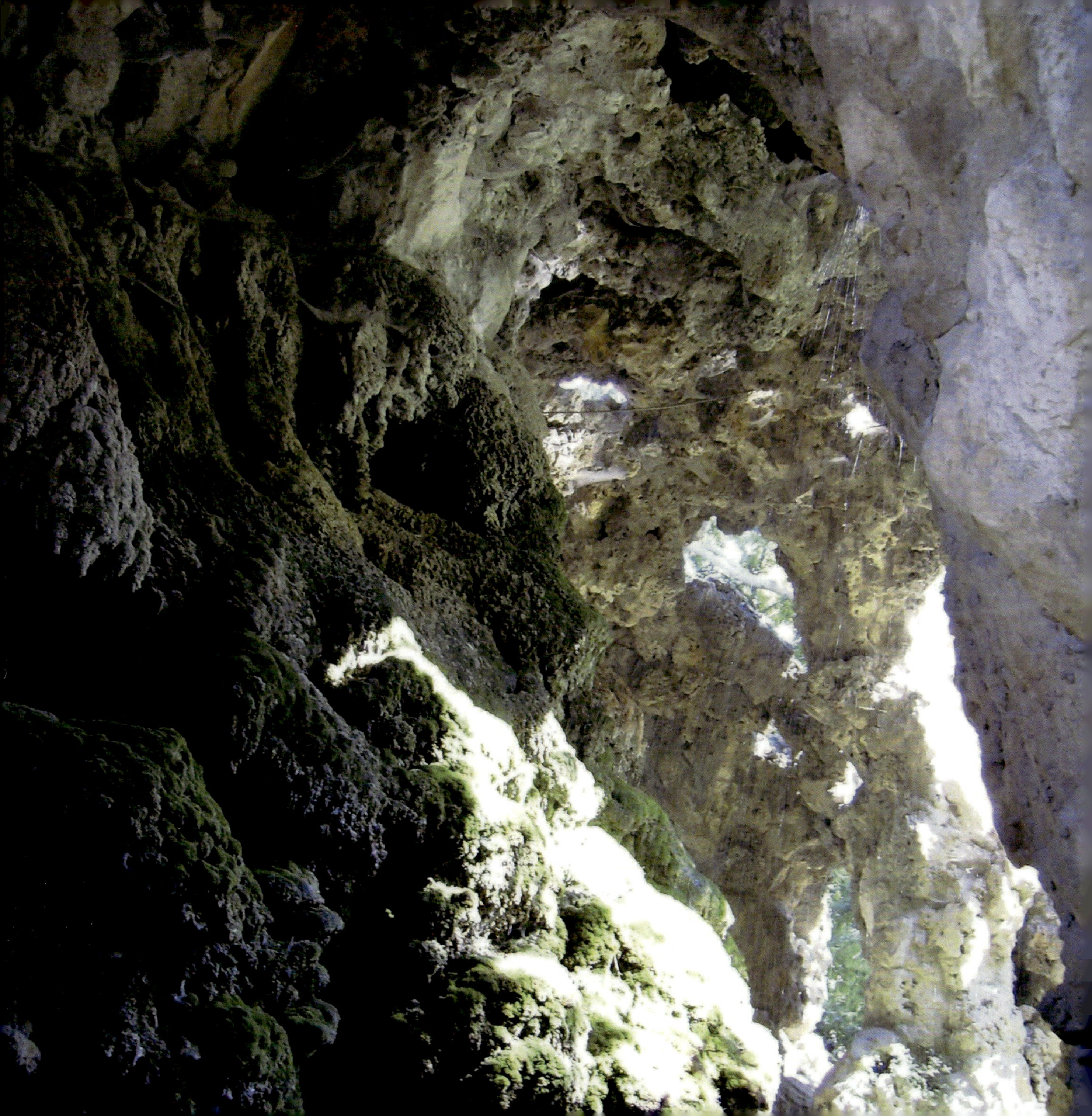

IMAGES OF THE CITY

Photo no. 2: "Tulip Hills"

by Veronika Bernard

Meran, 2012

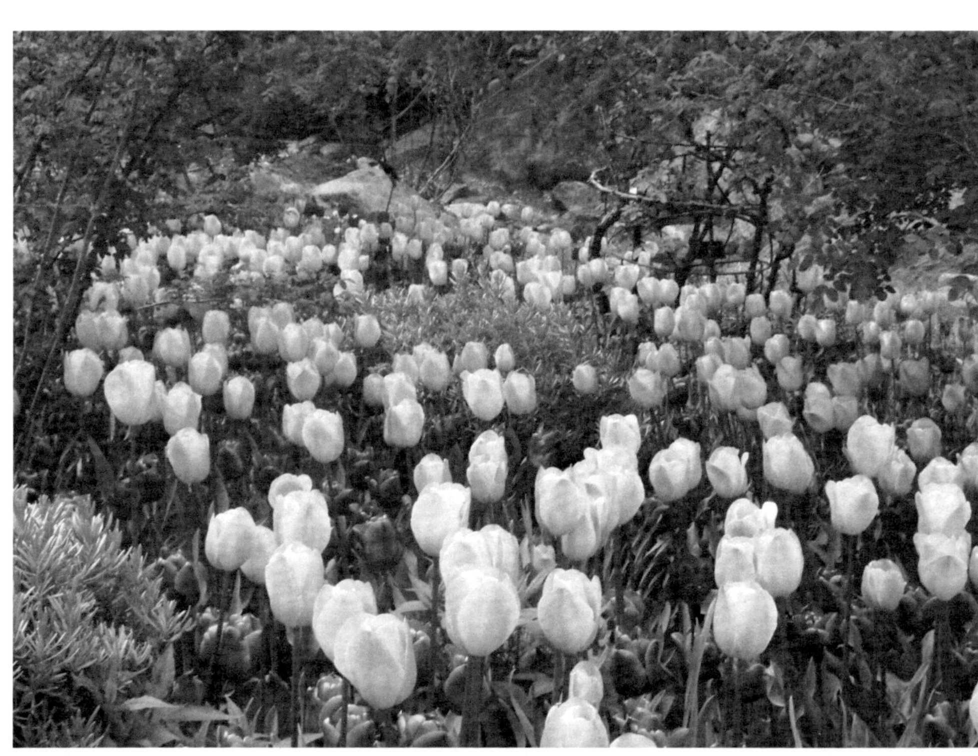

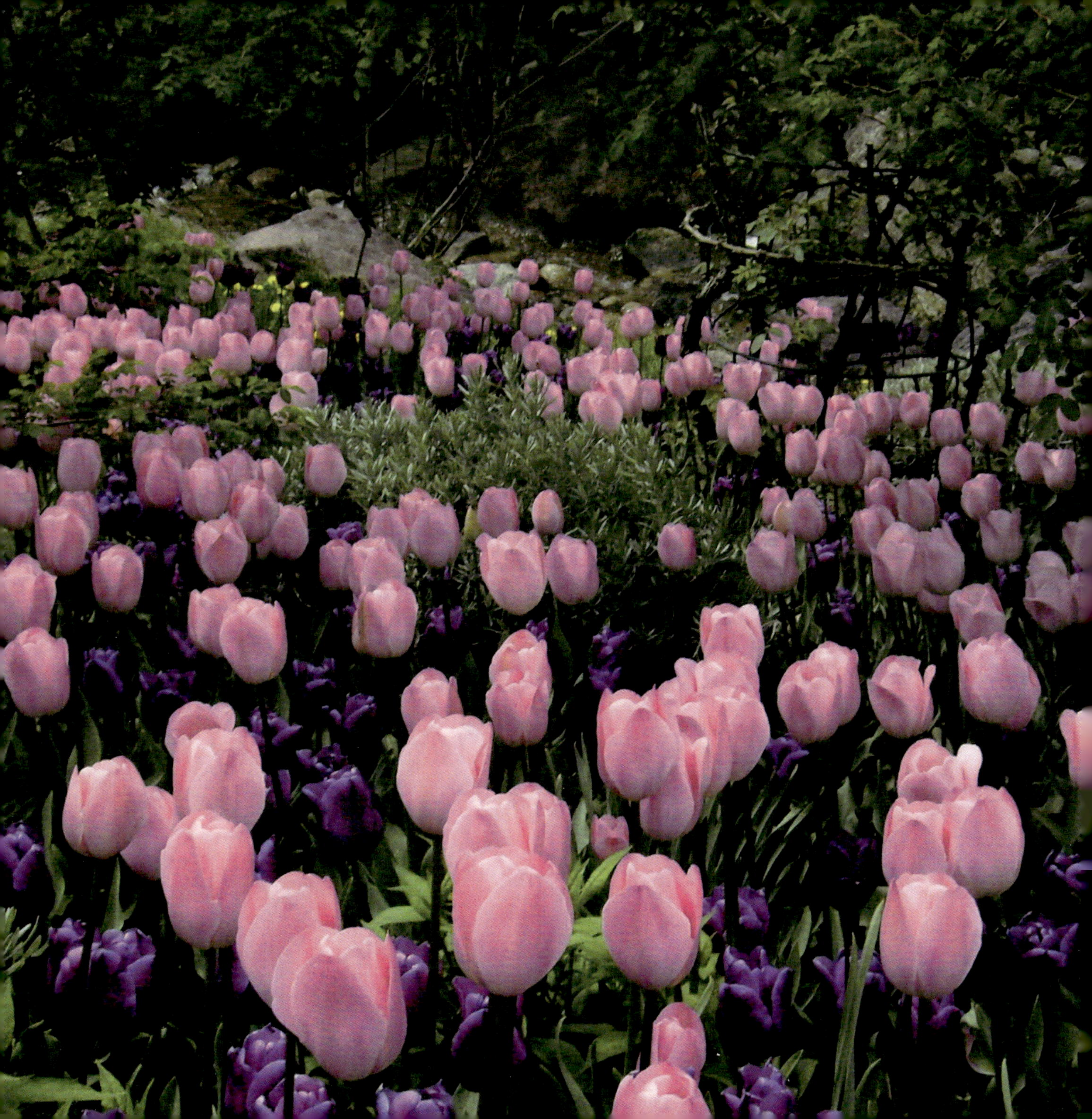

IMAGES OF THE CITY

Photo no. 3: "Ornamental Park Spring"

by Veronika Bernard

Istanbul (Emirgan Park, Tulip Festival), 2012

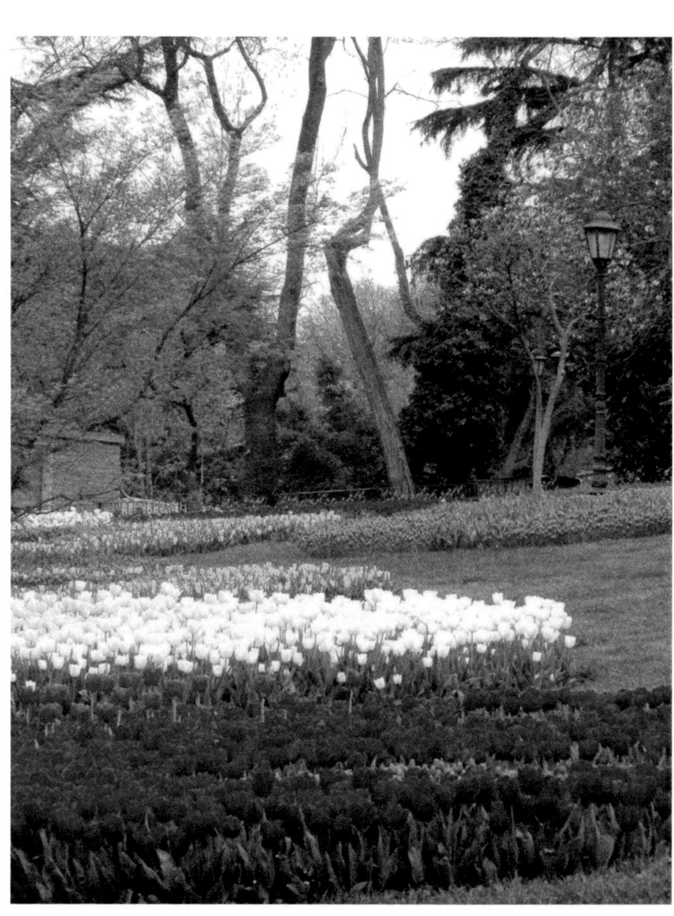

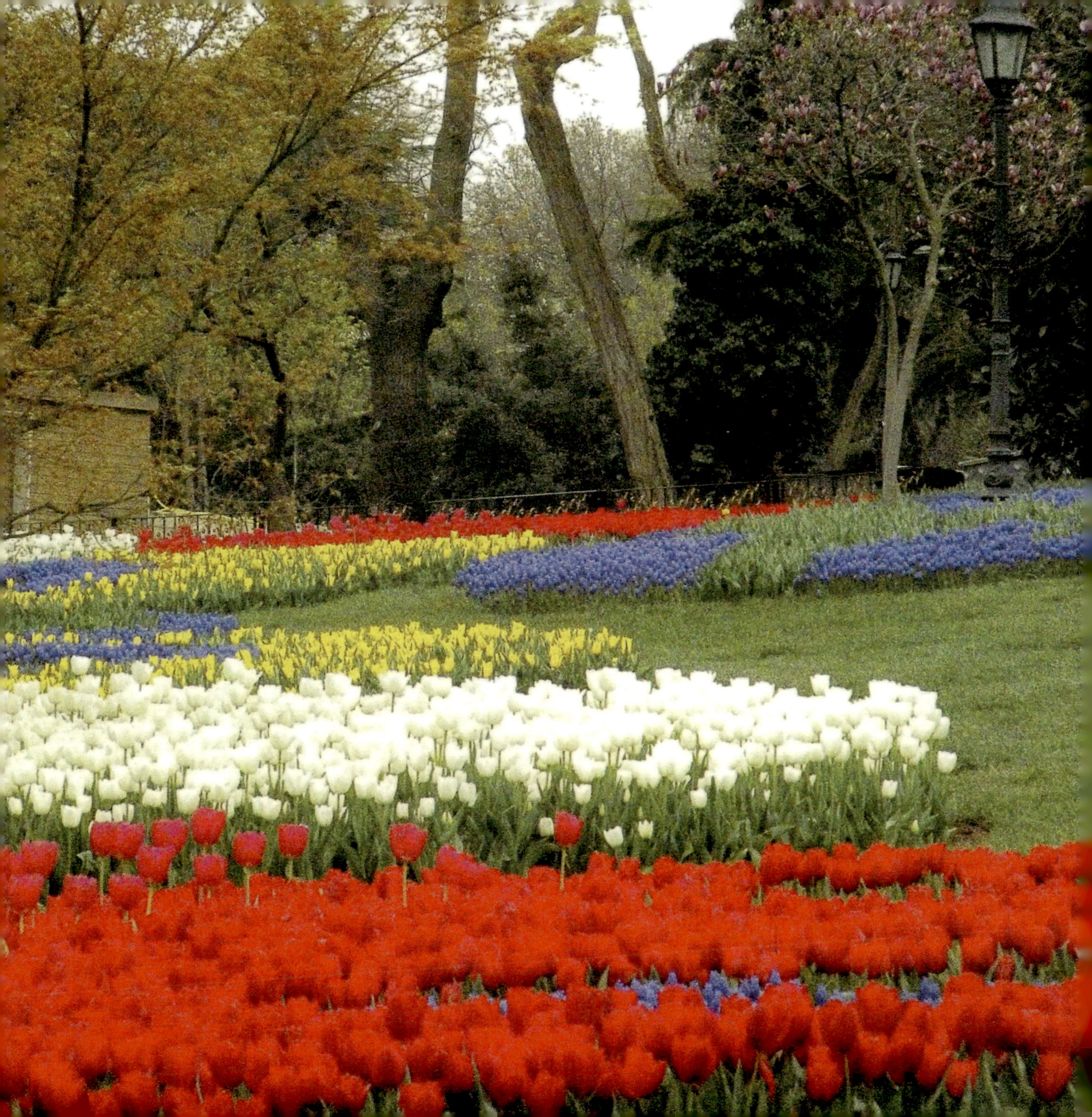

IMAGES OF THE CITY

Photo no. 4: "Fish for Joy"

by Veronika Bernard

Avignon, 2011

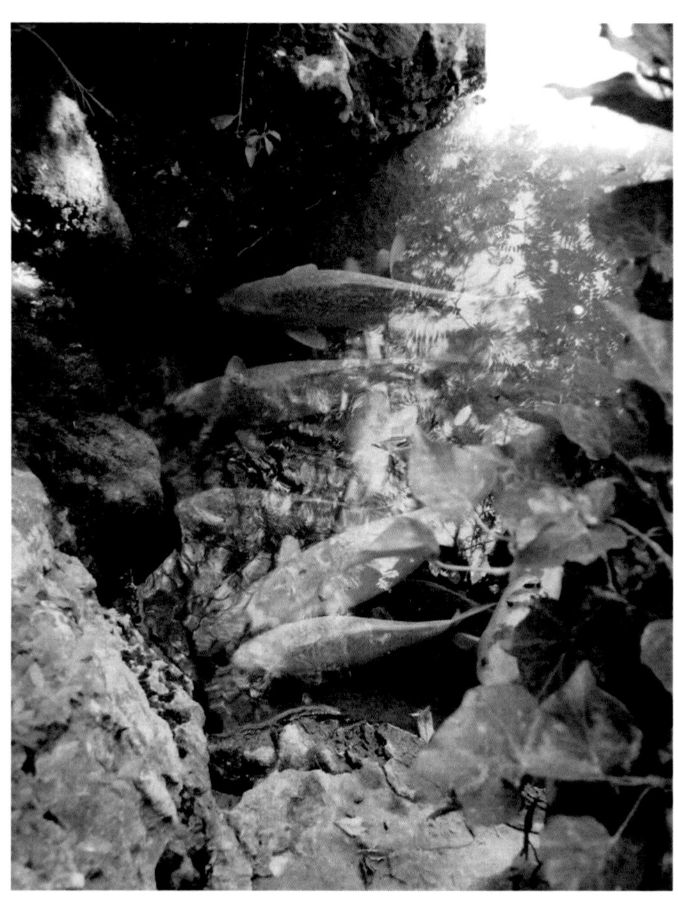

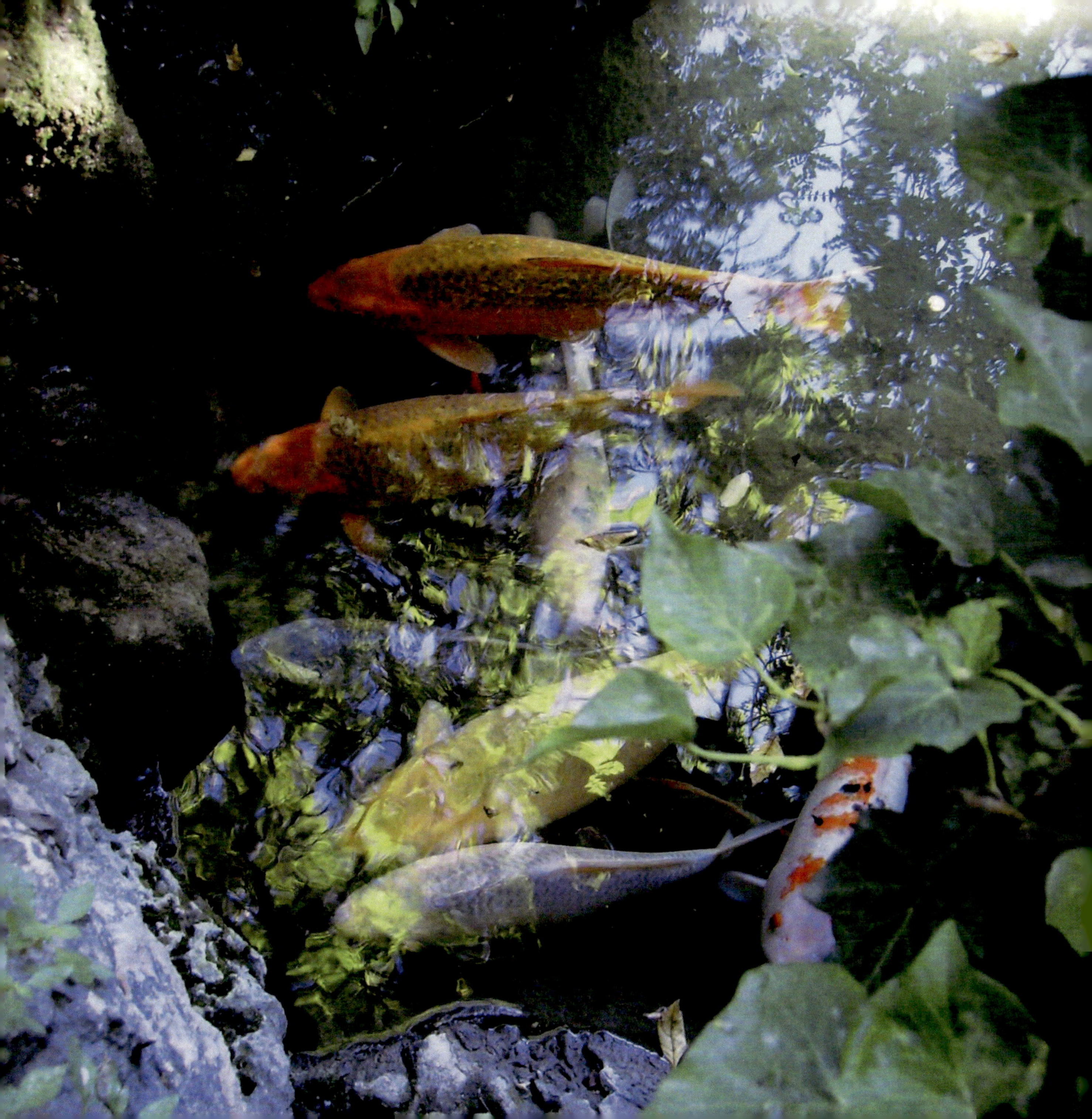

IMAGES OF THE CITY

Photo no. 5: "Water Choreography"

by Veronika Bernard

Bratislava, 2013

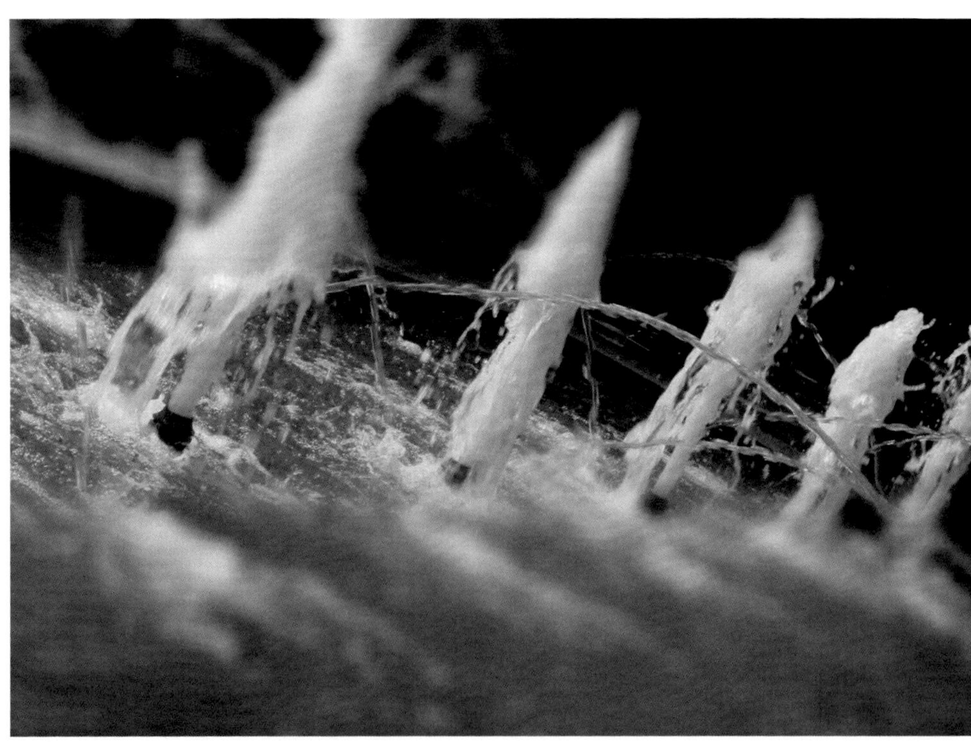

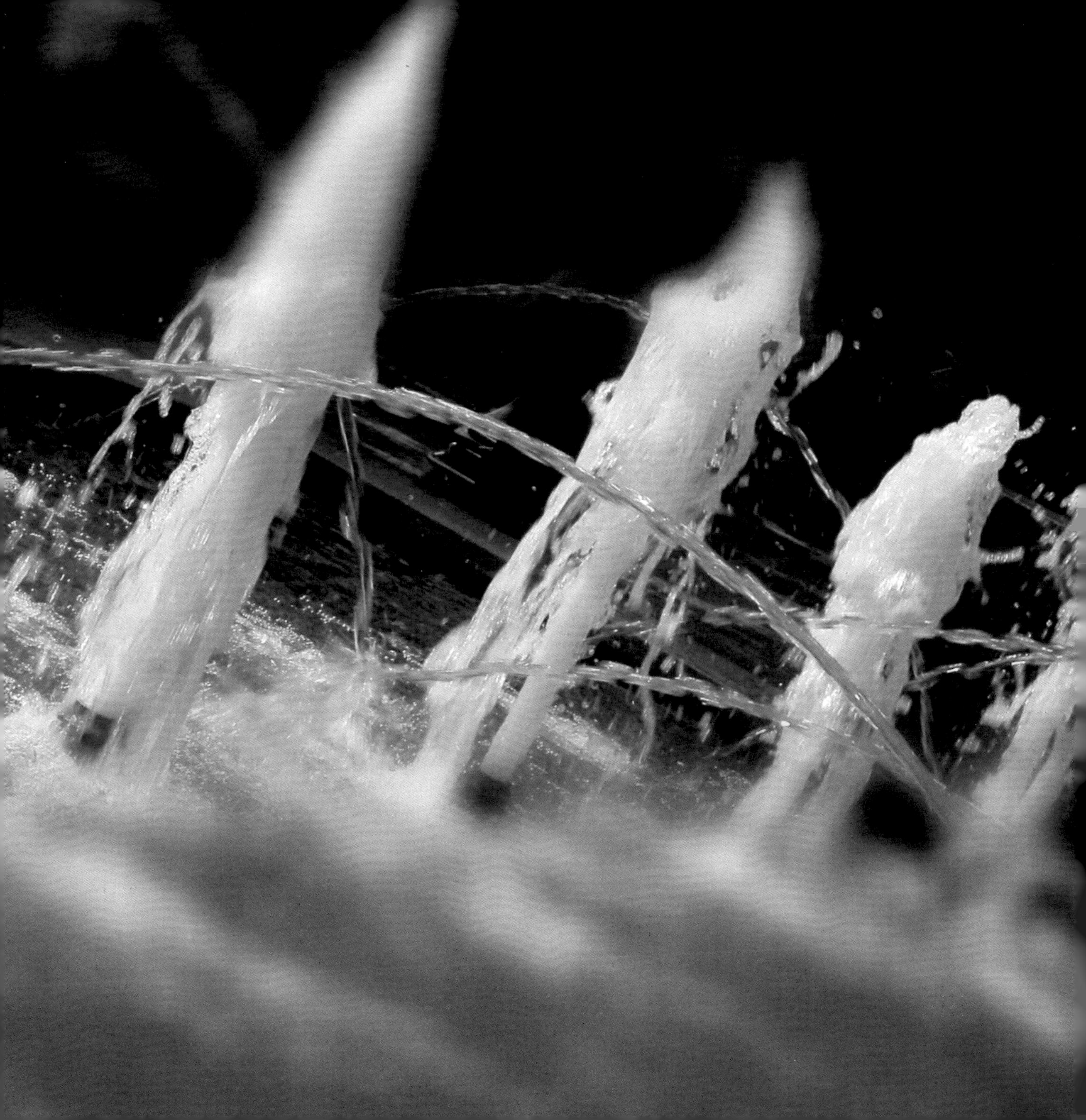

Urban Architecture

Urbane Architektur

IMAGES OF THE CITY

Photo no. 6: "Colour Architecture"

by Veronika Bernard

Cologne (Elisabeth-Treskow-Platz), 2013

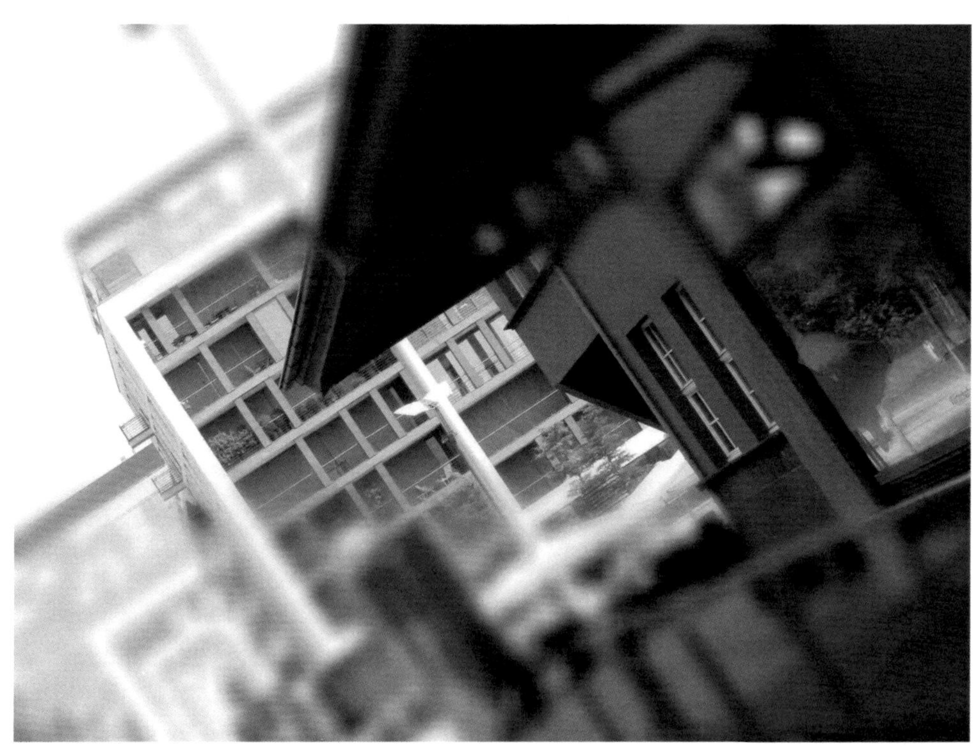

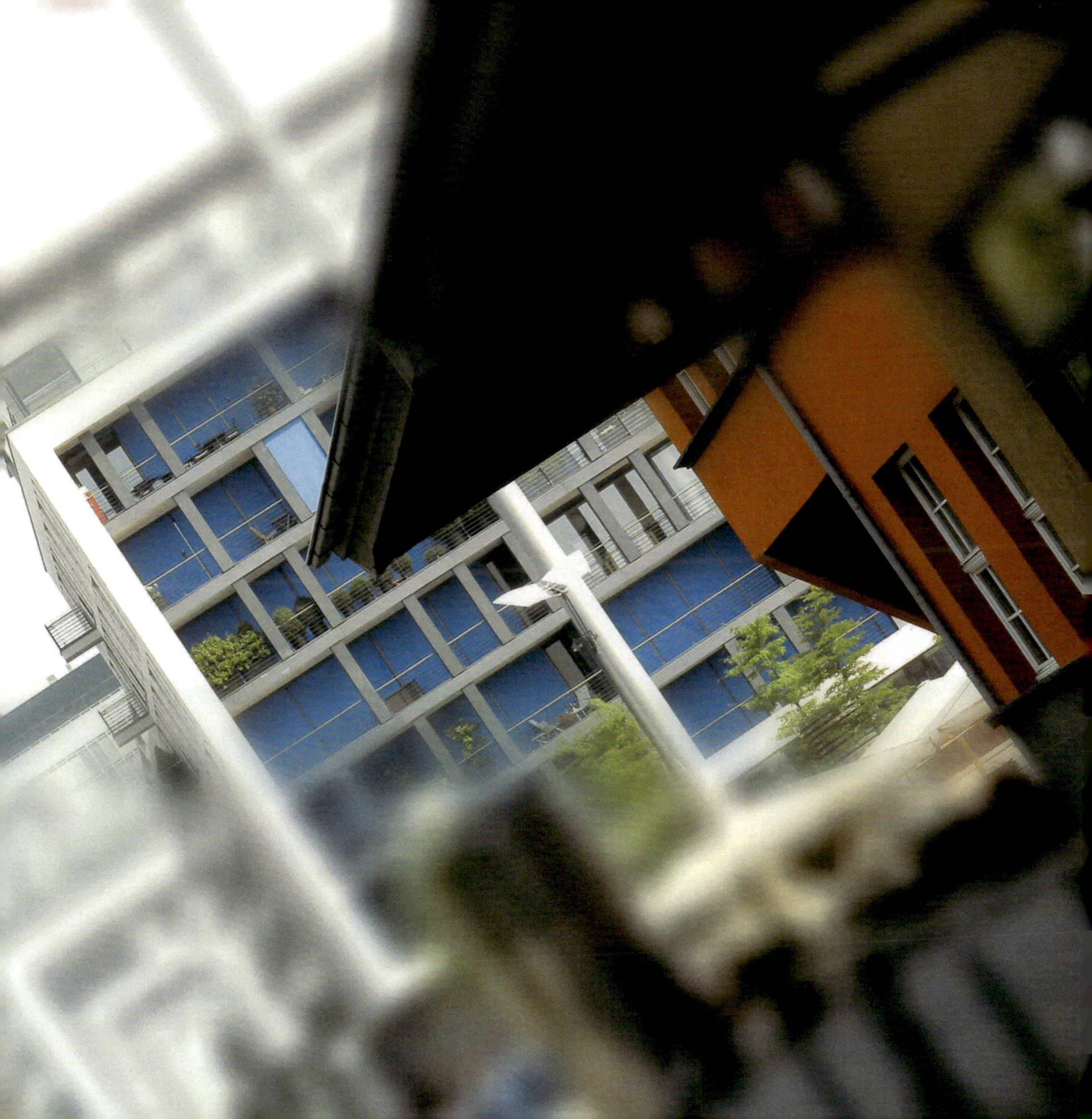

IMAGES OF THE CITY

Photo no. 7: "Urban Neighbours"

by Veronika Bernard

Cologne, 2013

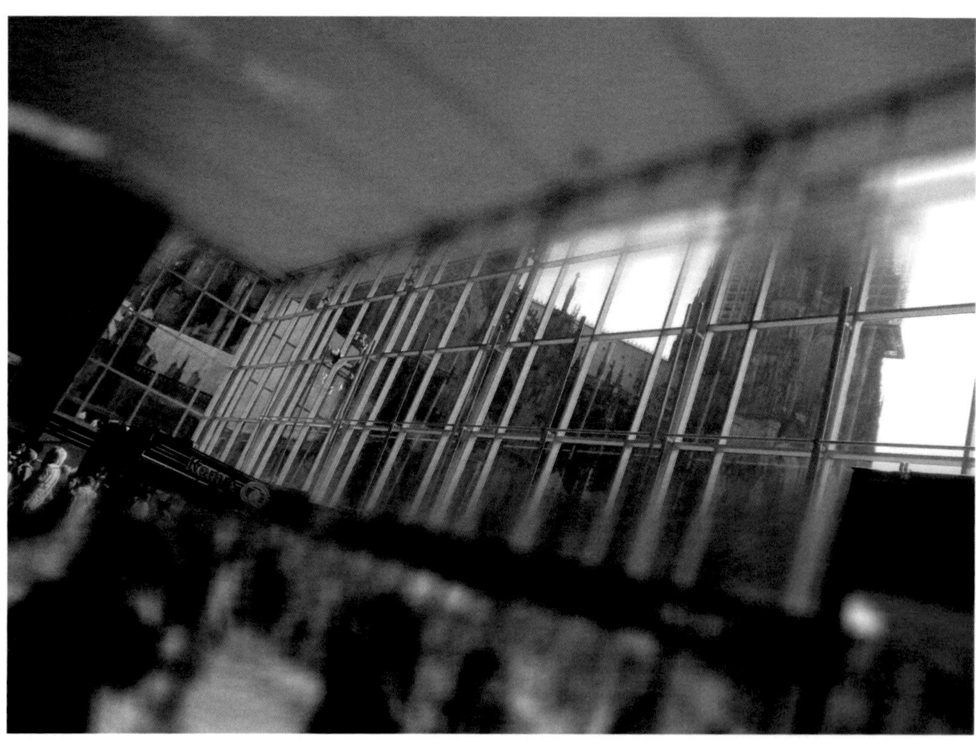

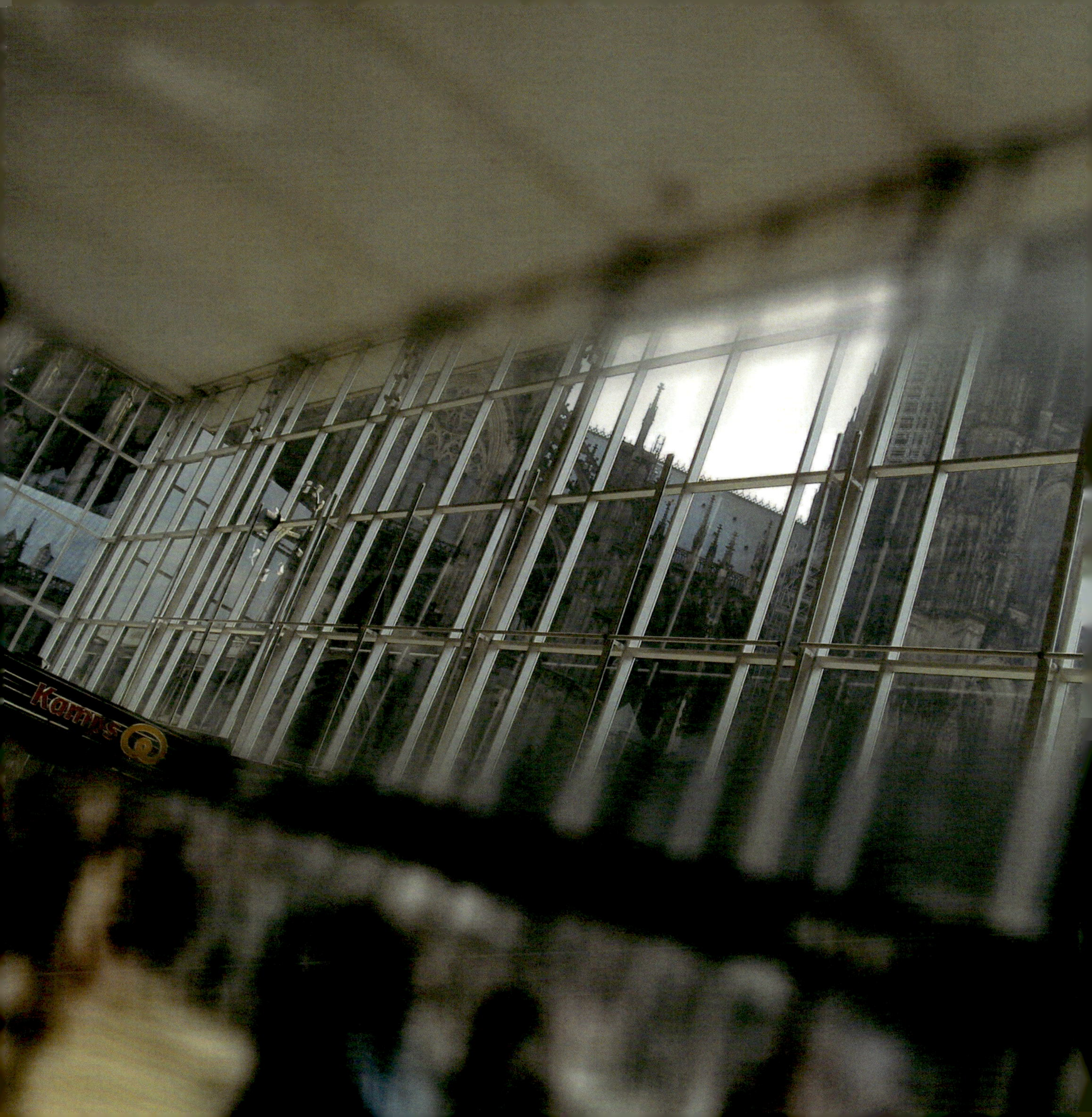

IMAGES OF THE CITY

Photo no. 8: "Contrasts"

by Veronika Bernard

Berlin (Potsdamer Platz), 2012

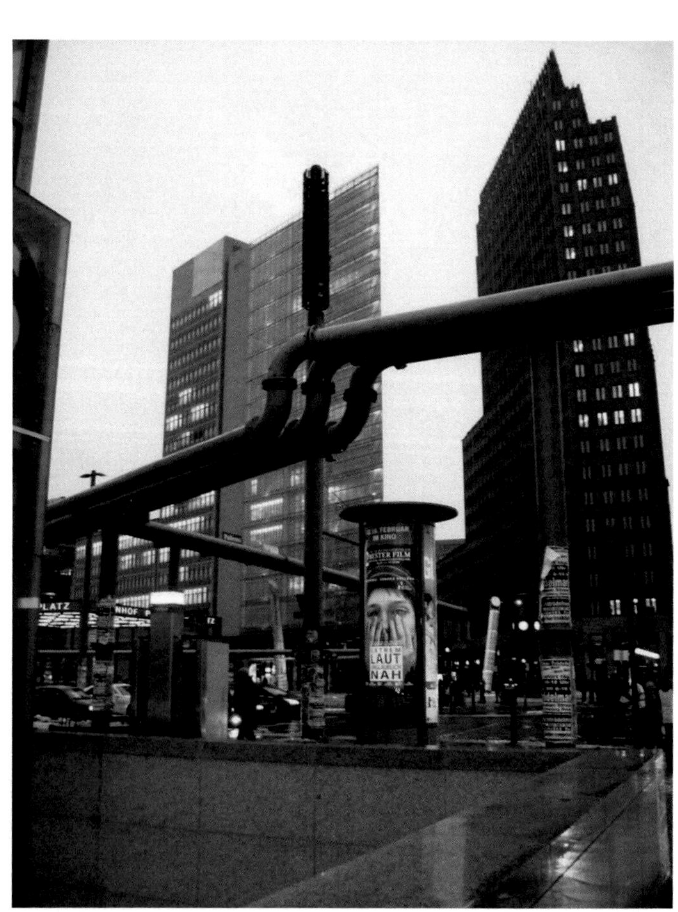

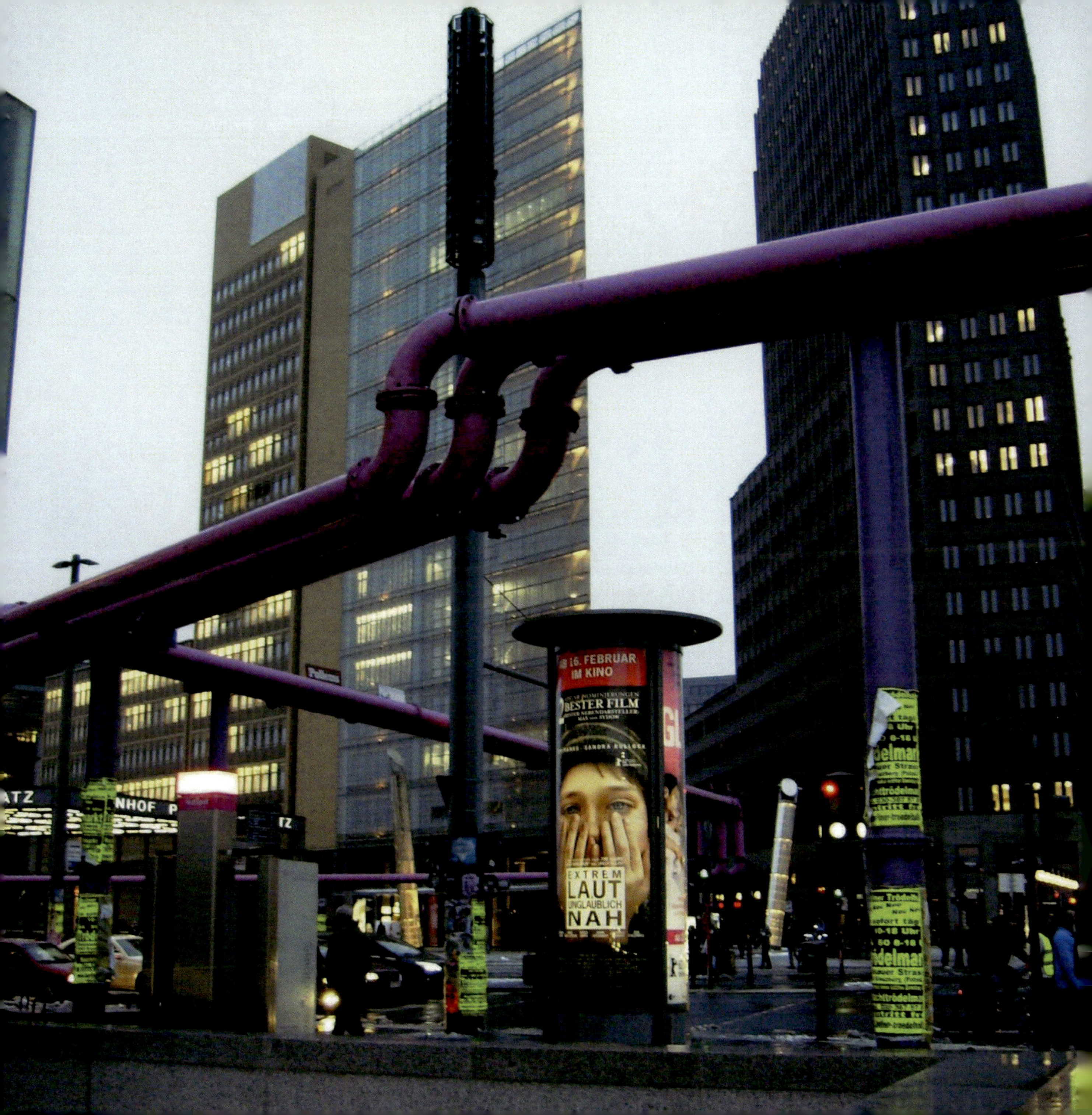

16. FEBRUAR
IM KINO
BESTER FILM
EXTREM
LAUT
UNGLAUBLICH
NAH

IMAGES OF THE CITY

Photo no. 9: "Bricks & Colours"

by Veronika Bernard

Cologne (Rheinauhafen), 2013

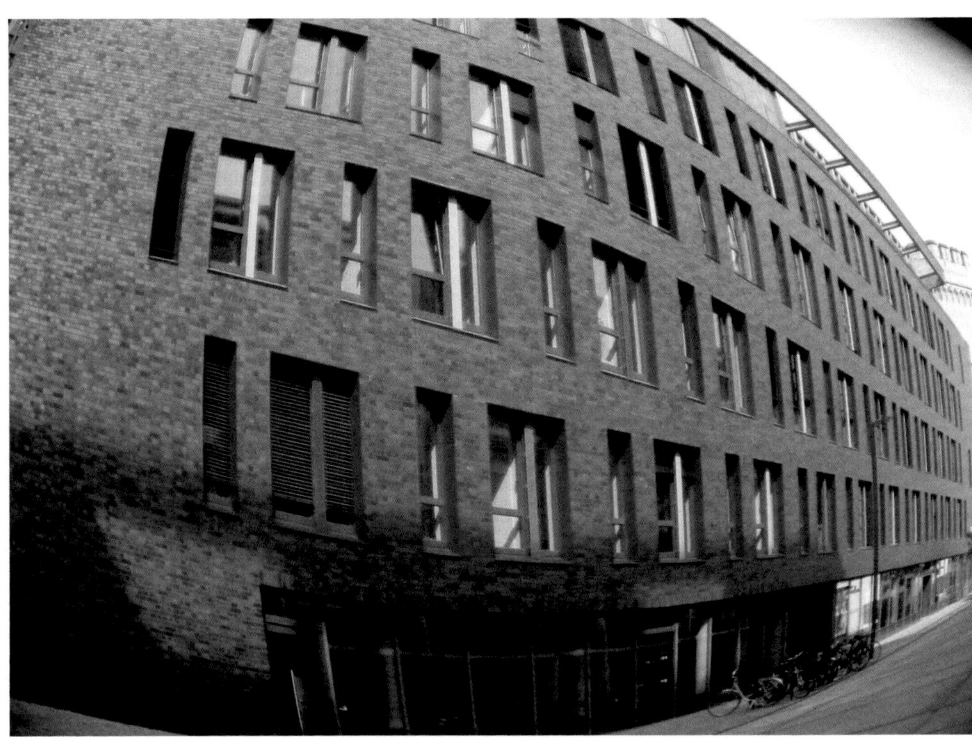

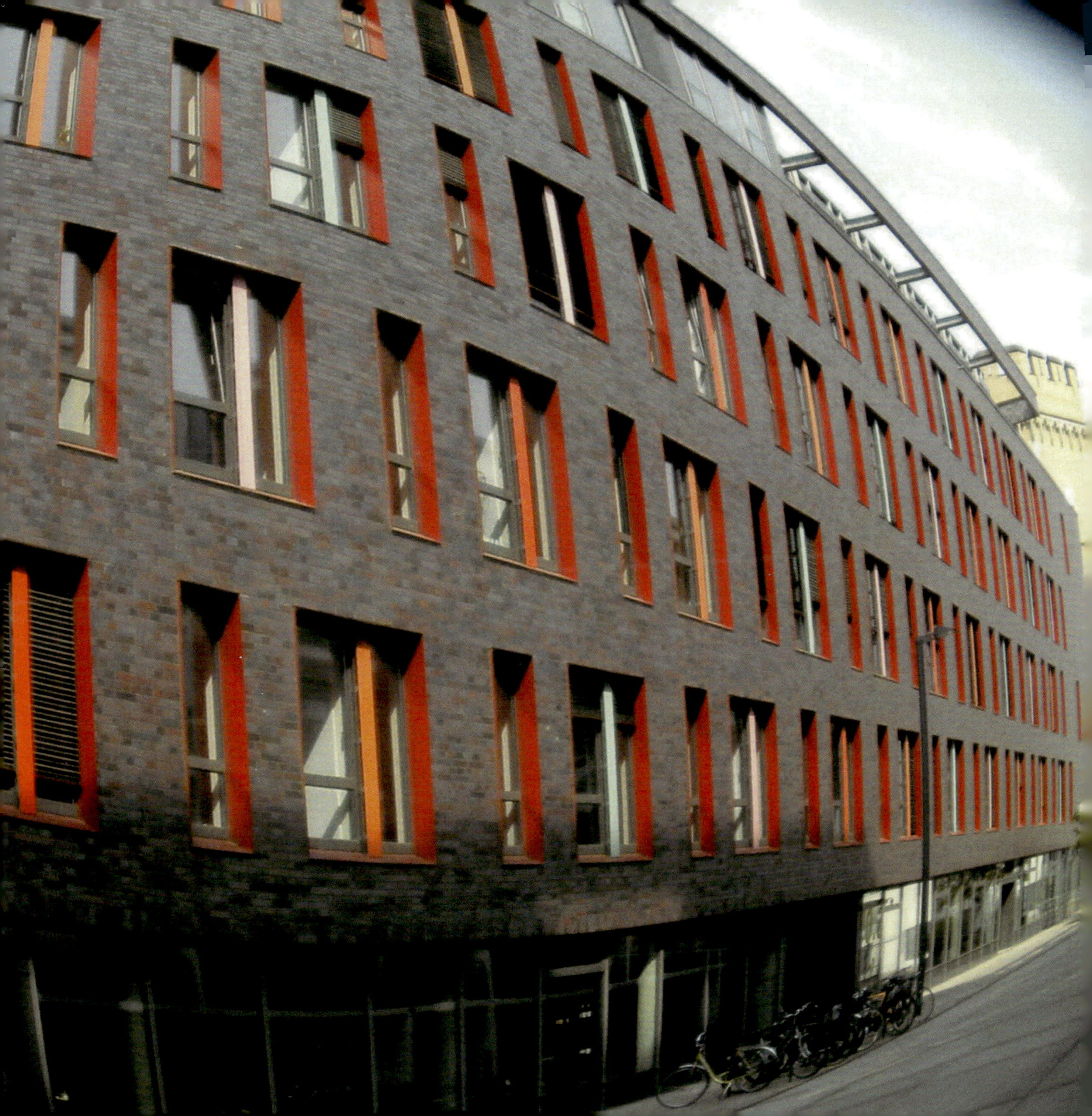

IMAGES OF THE CITY

Photo no.10: "Urban Statements & Messages"

by Veronika Bernard

Cologne (Rheinauhafen, Kranhäuser), 2013

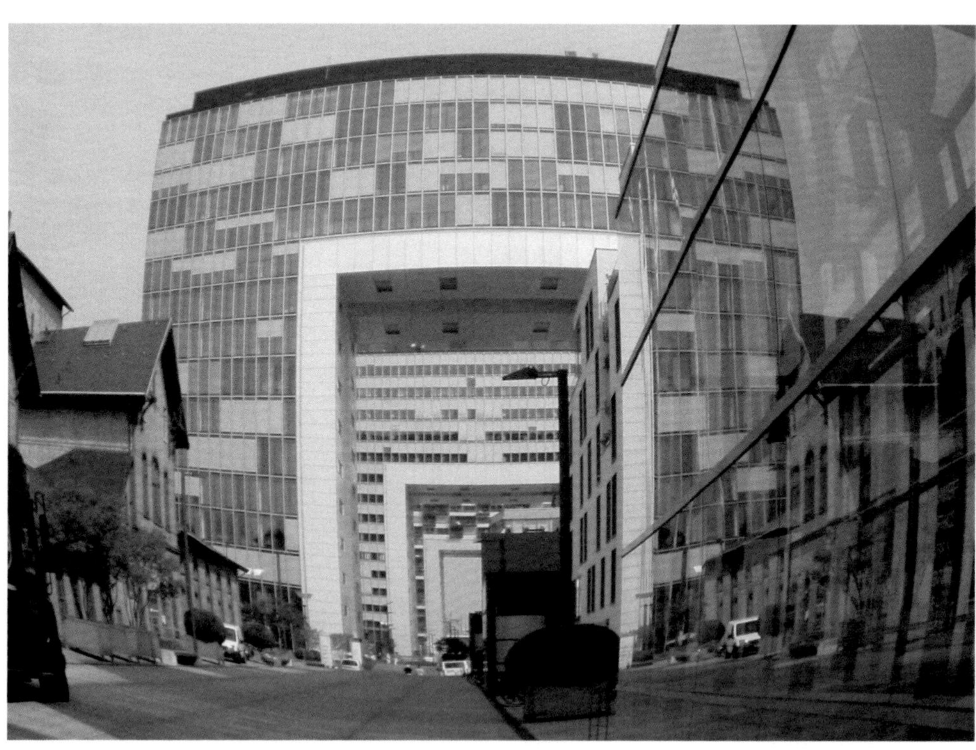

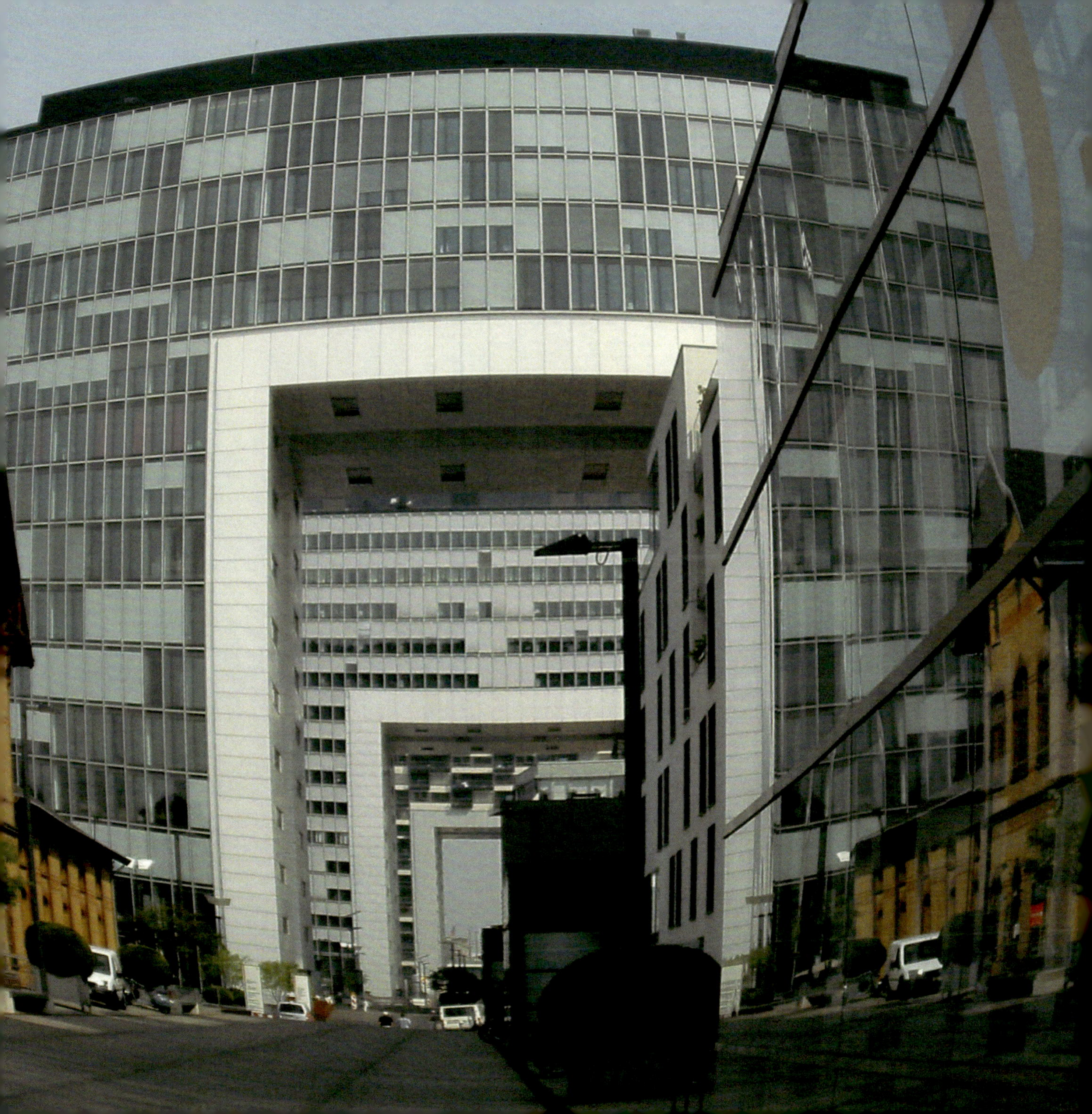

IMAGES OF THE CITY

Photo no. 11: "Golden Past"

by Veronika Bernard

Budapest, 2013

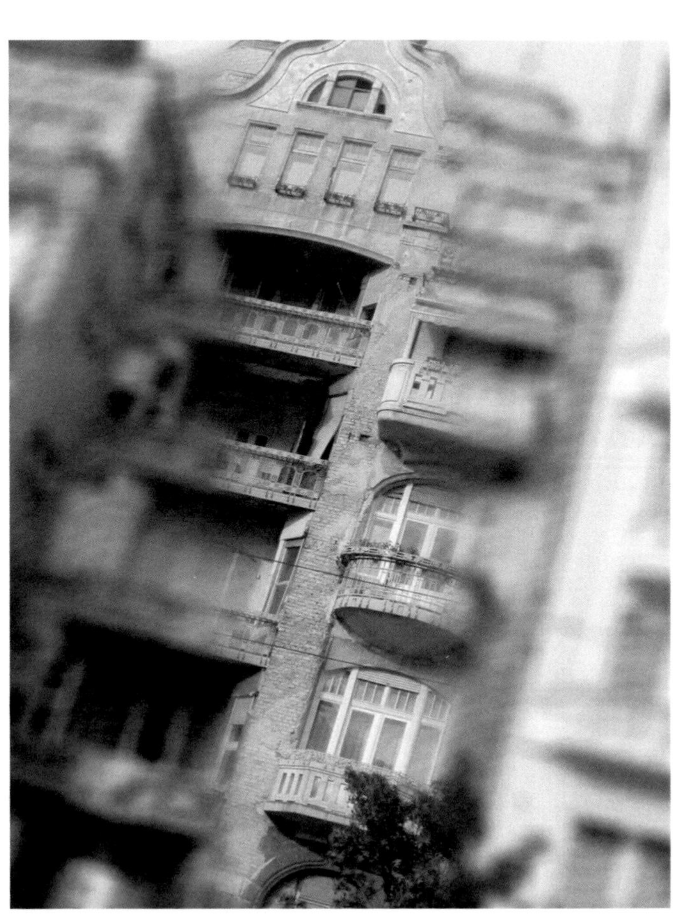

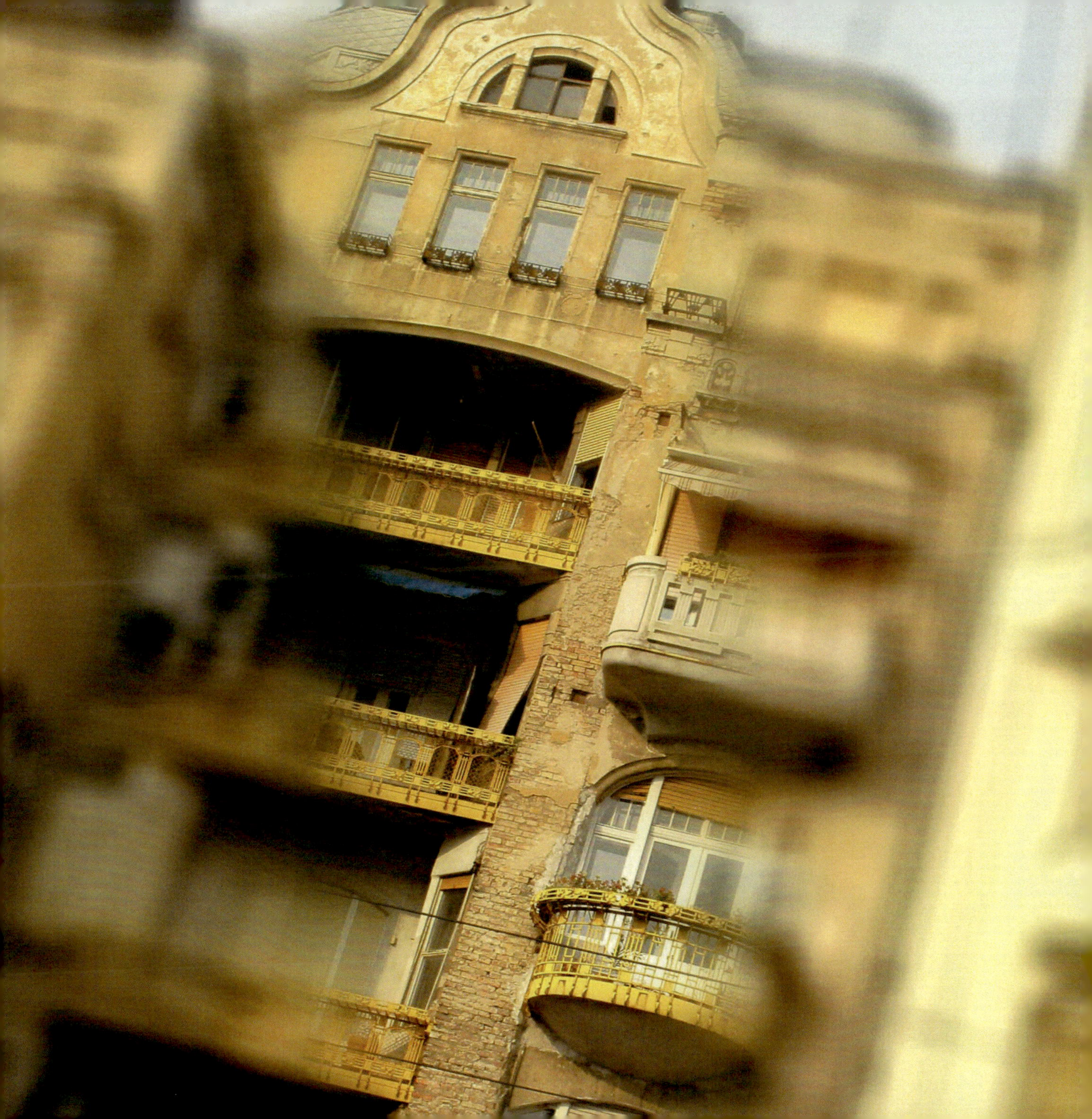

IMAGES OF THE CITY

Photo no. 12: "The Beauty of Iron and Colours"

by Veronika Bernard

Budapest, 2013

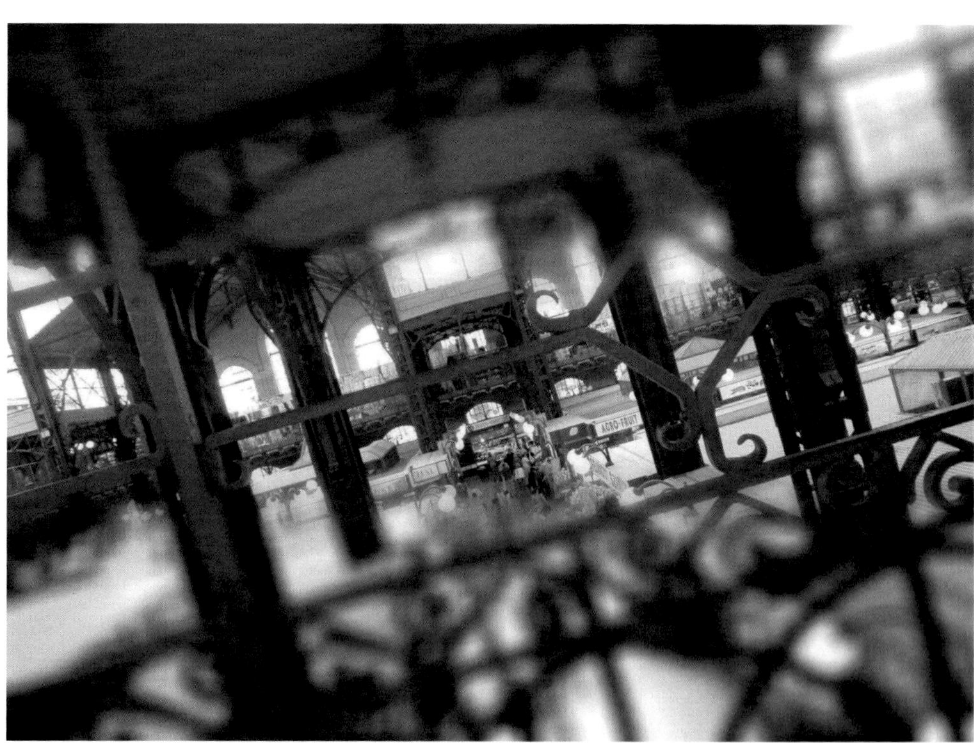

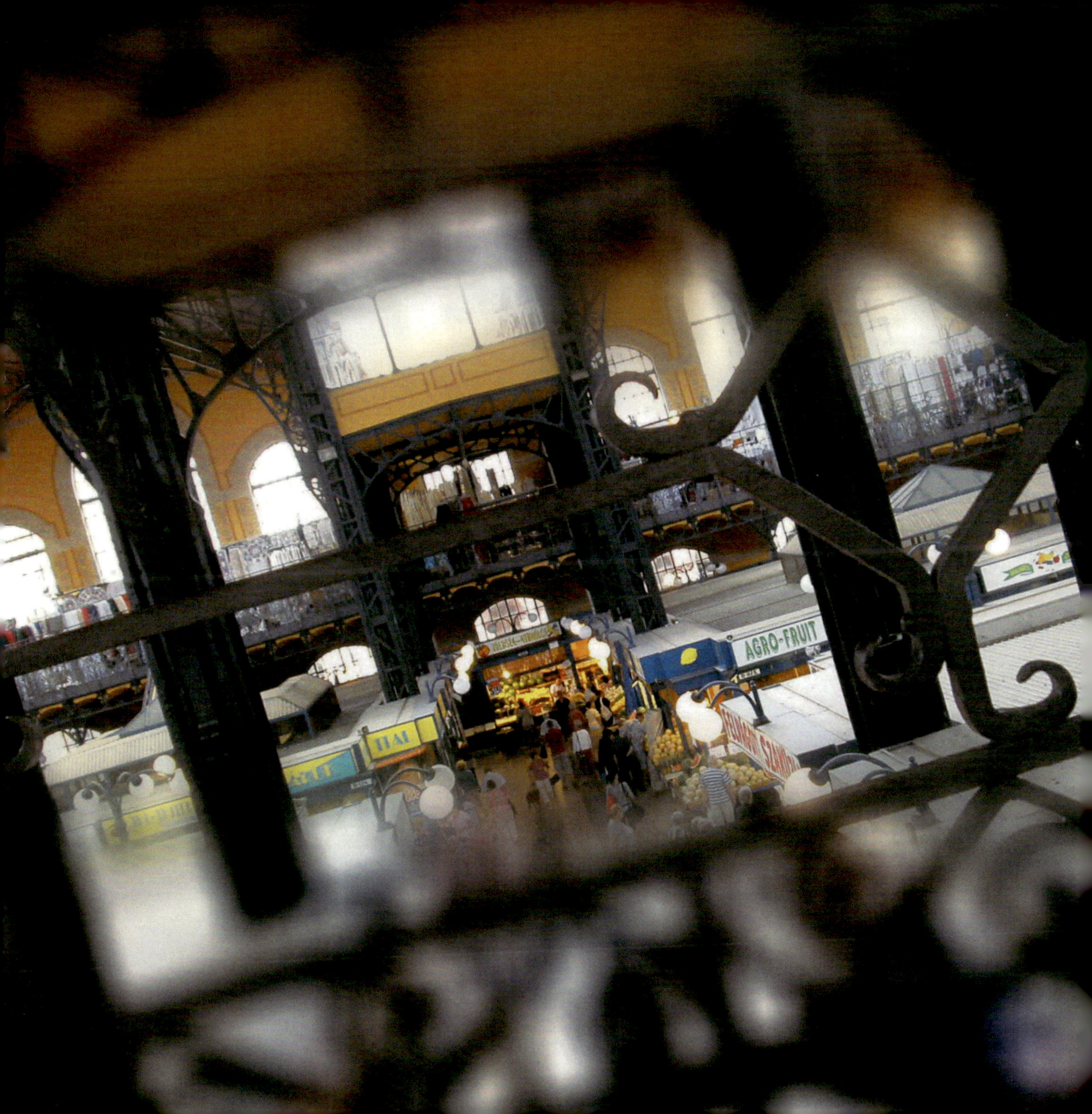
AGRO-FRUIT

IMAGES OF THE CITY

Photo no. 13: "Crossing Waters"

by Veronika Bernard

Lyon, 2011

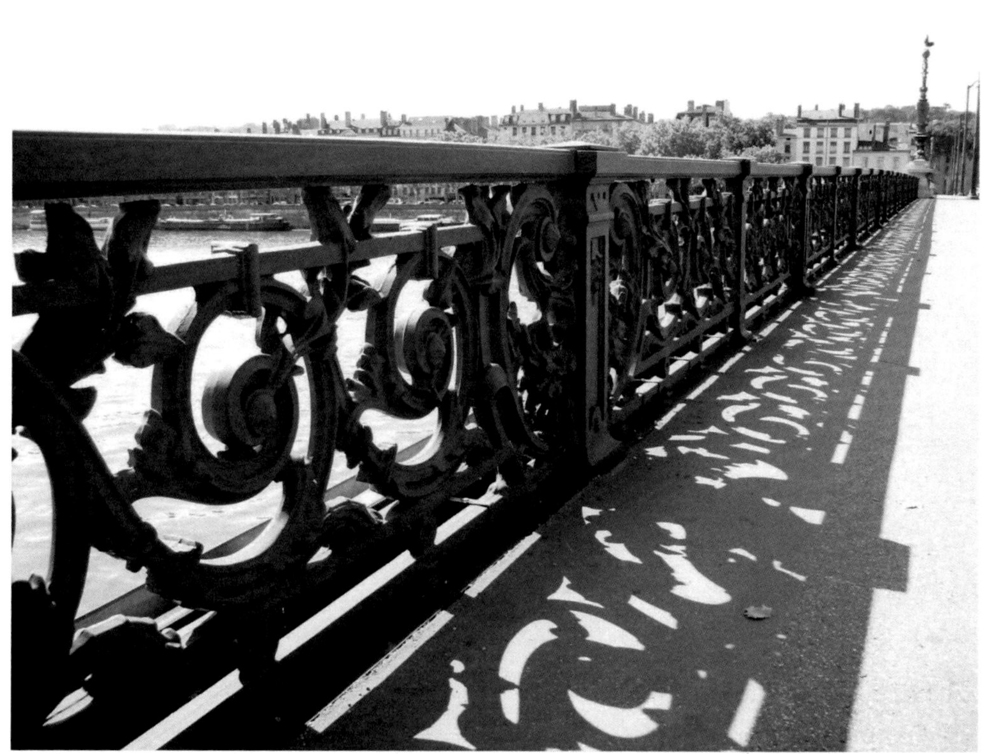

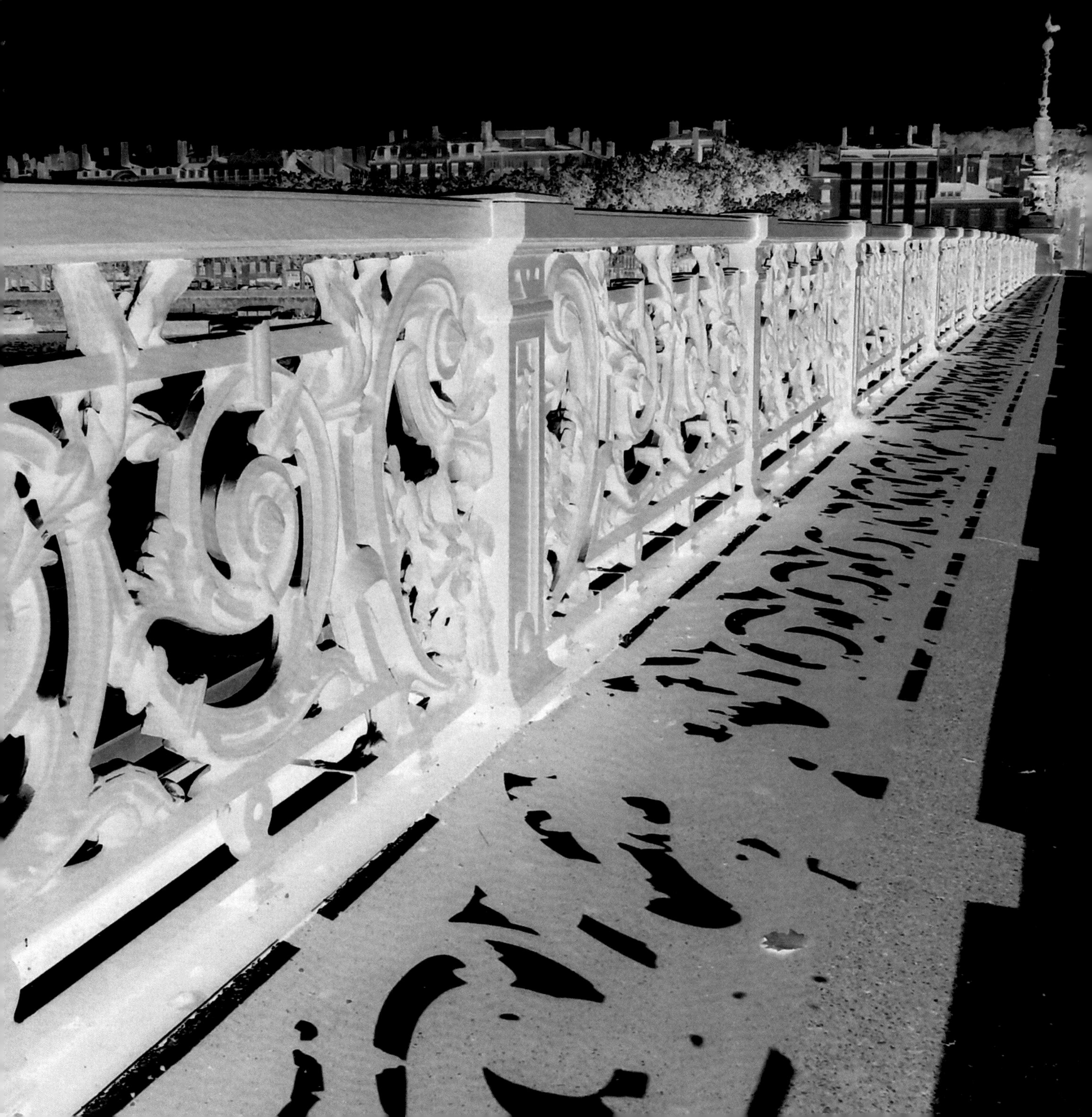

IMAGES OF THE CITY

Photo no. 14: "Modernity & Tradition"

by Veronika Bernard

Mainz, 2012

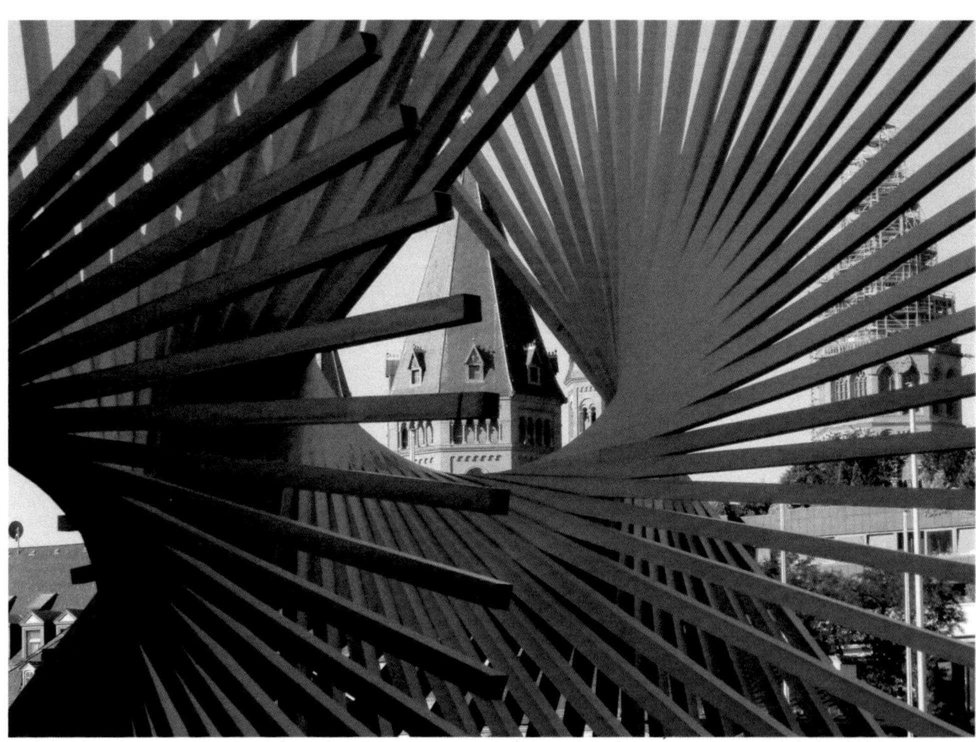

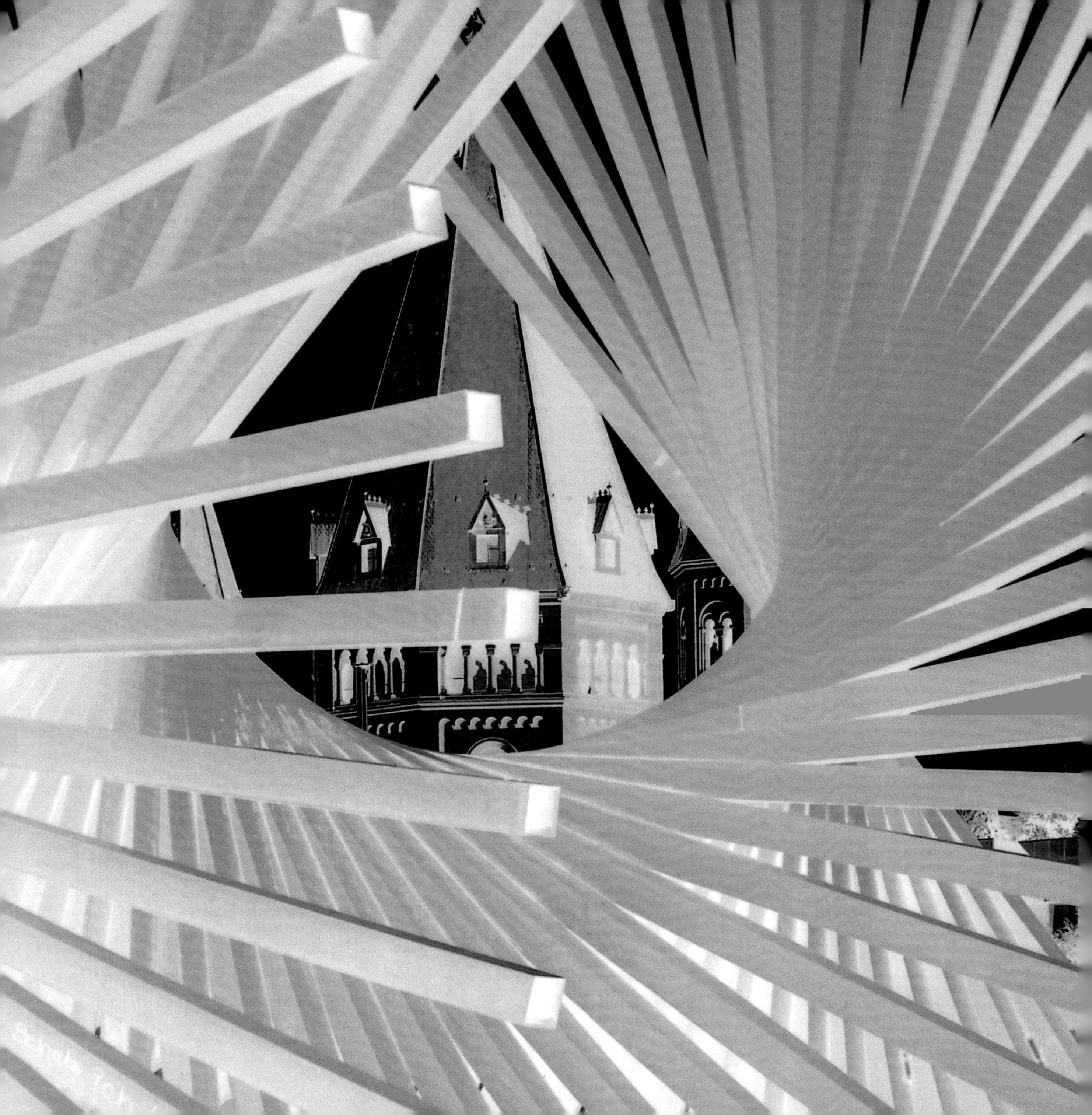

IMAGES OF THE CITY

Photo no. 15: "Riverside Harbour Look"

by Veronika Bernard

Cologne (Agrippinwerft), 2013

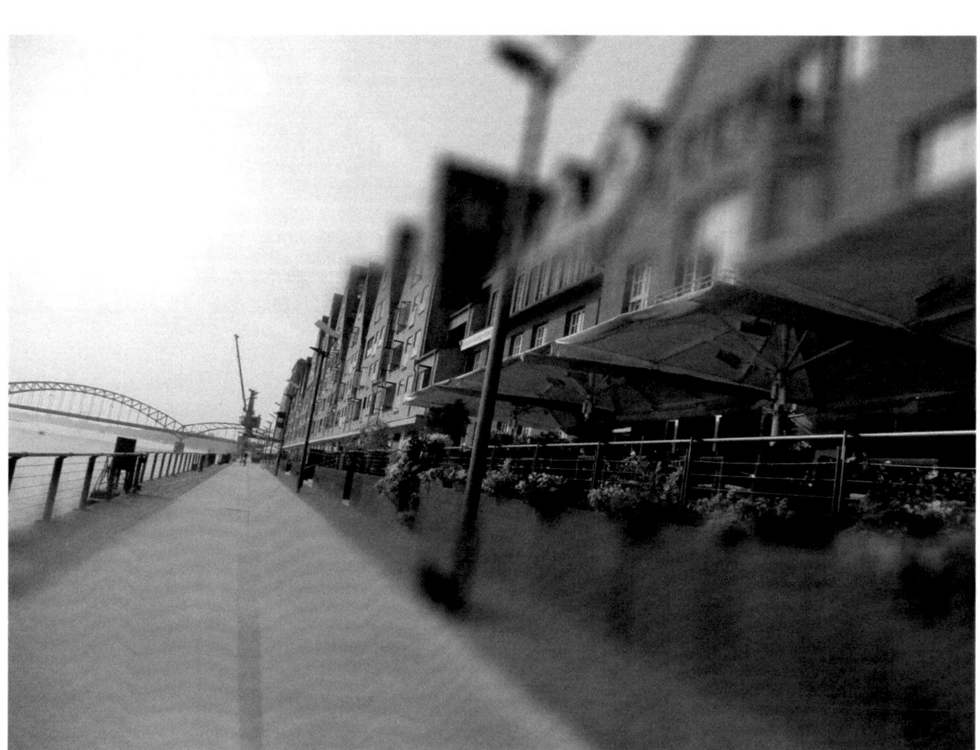

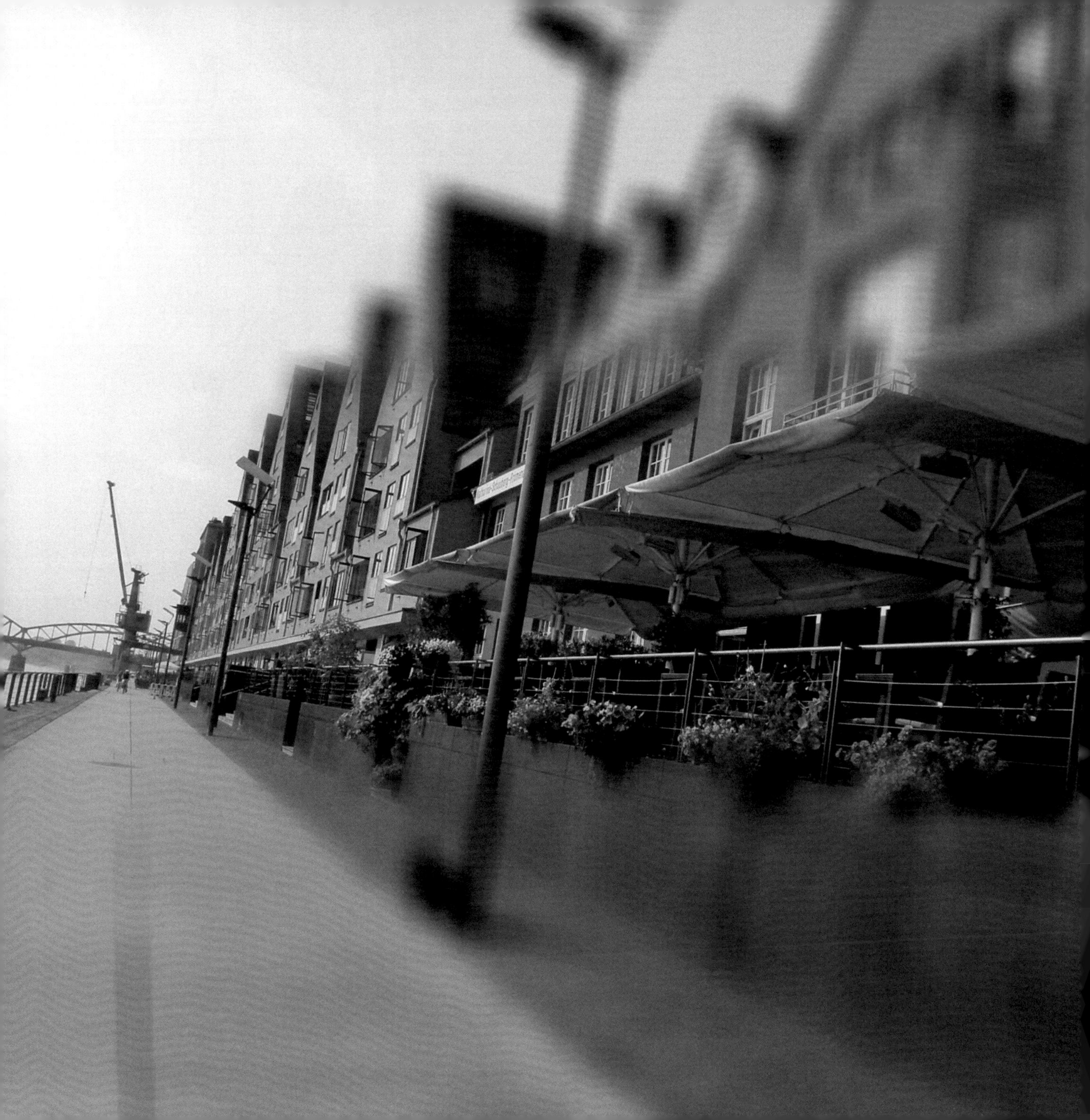

IMAGES OF THE CITY

Photo no. 16: "Façades in Pouring Rain"

by Veronika Bernard

Lyon, 2011

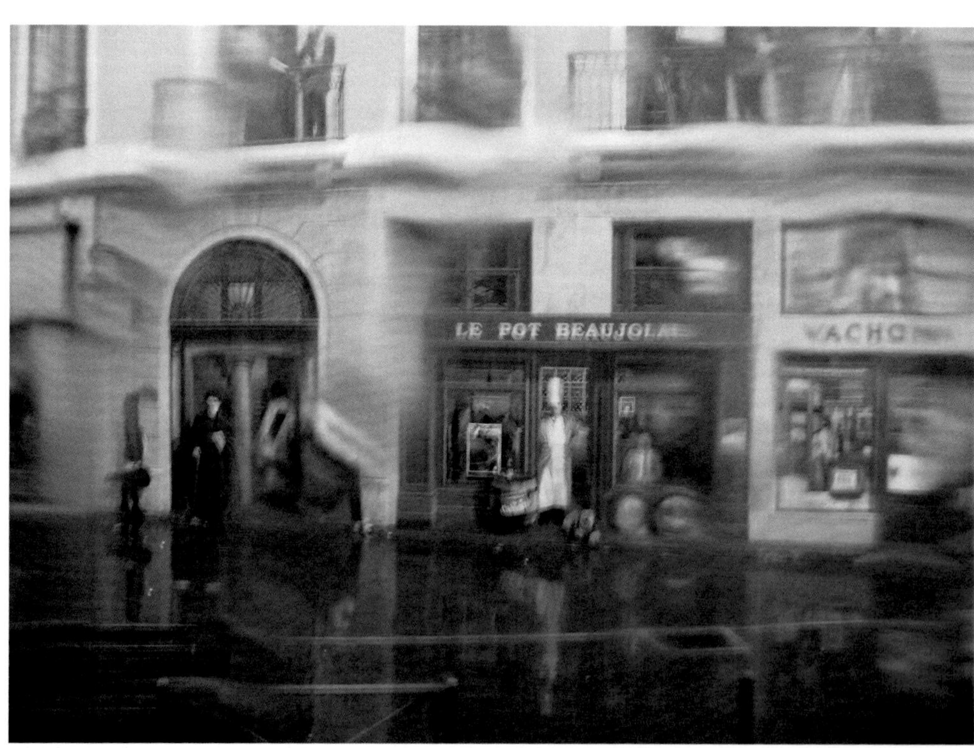

LE POT BEAUJOL

IMAGES OF THE CITY

Photo no. 17: "Sunlight Architecture"

by Veronika Bernard

Cologne (Agrippinwerft), 2013

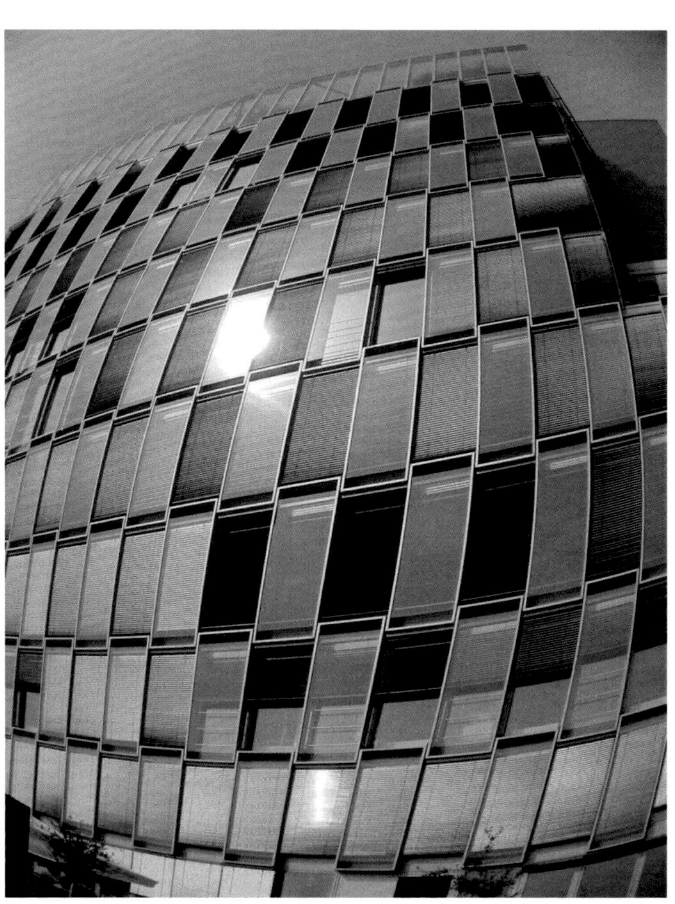

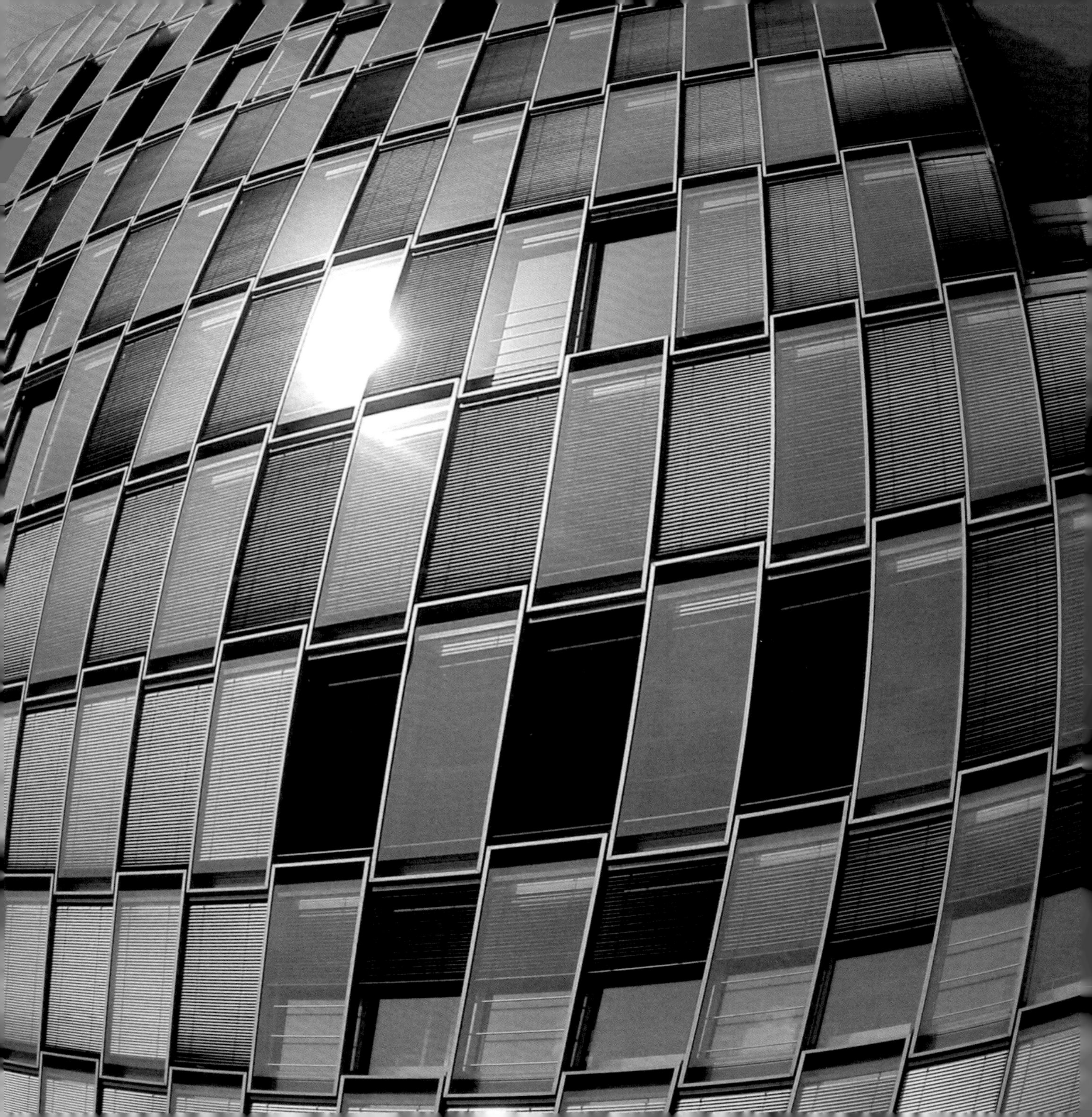

IMAGES OF THE CITY

Photo no. 18: "Looking up to"

by Veronika Bernard

Cologne (Rheinauhafen, Kranhäuser), 2013

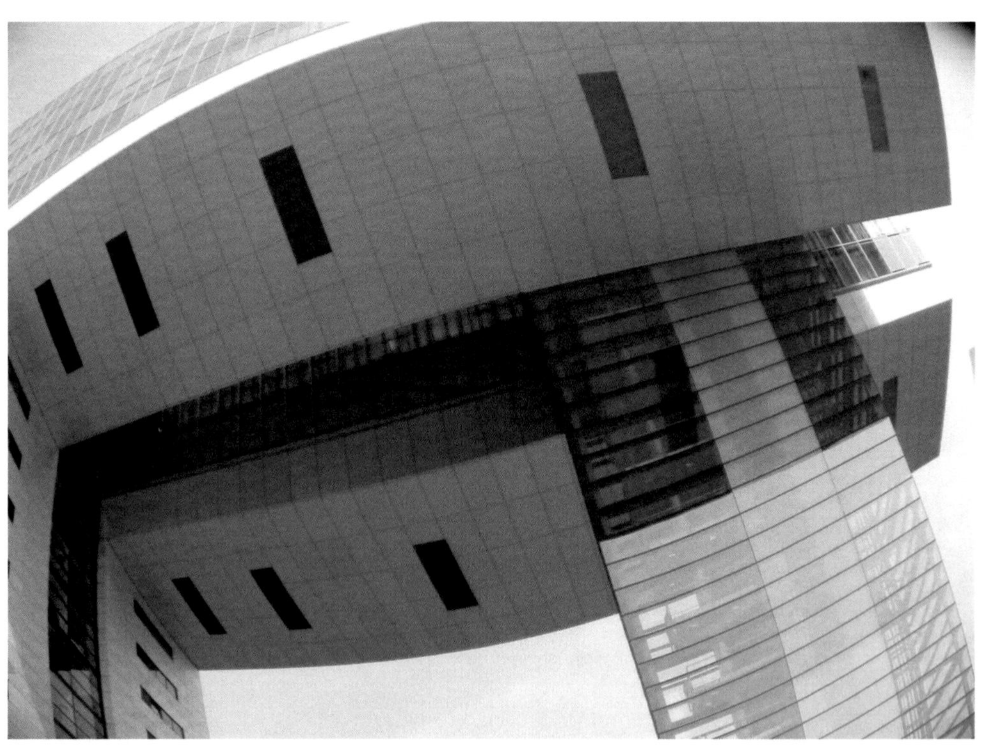

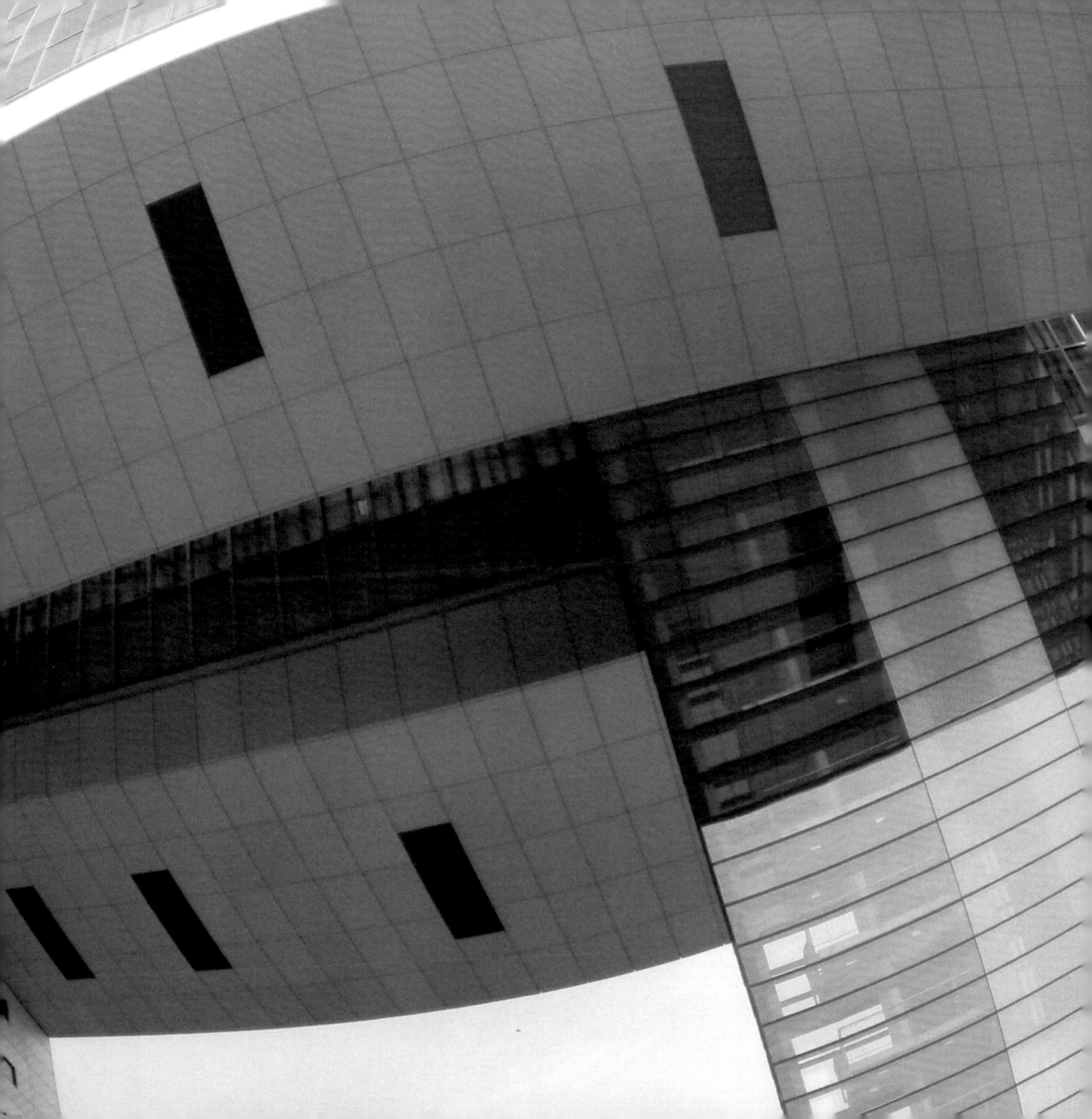

IMAGES OF THE CITY

Photo no. 19: "Beautiful Protection"

by Veronika Bernard

Budapest, 2013

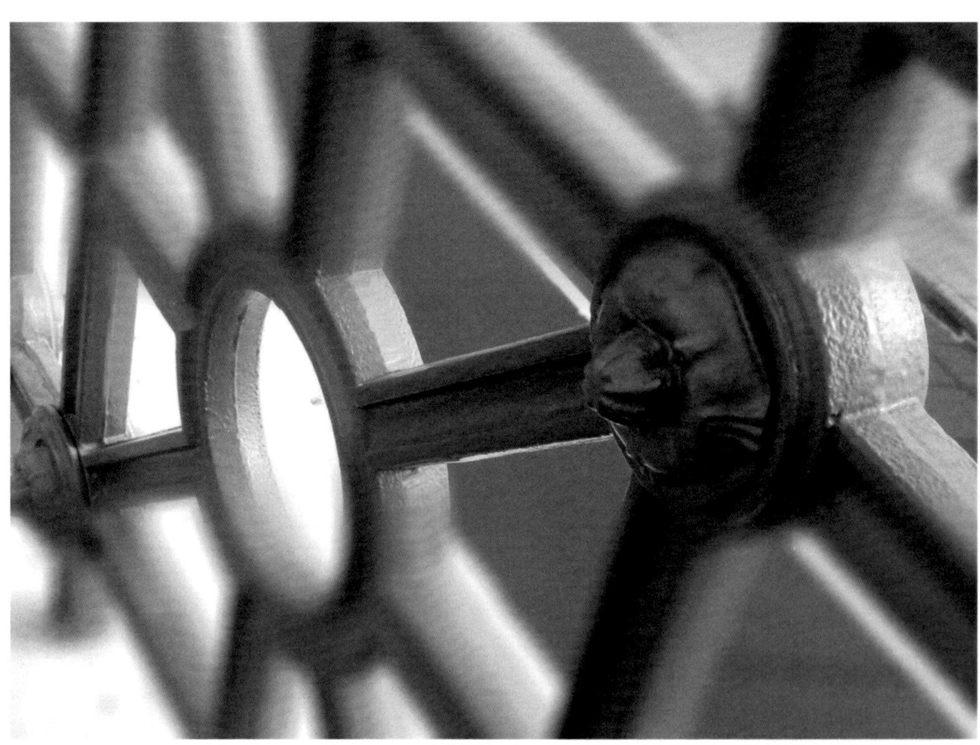

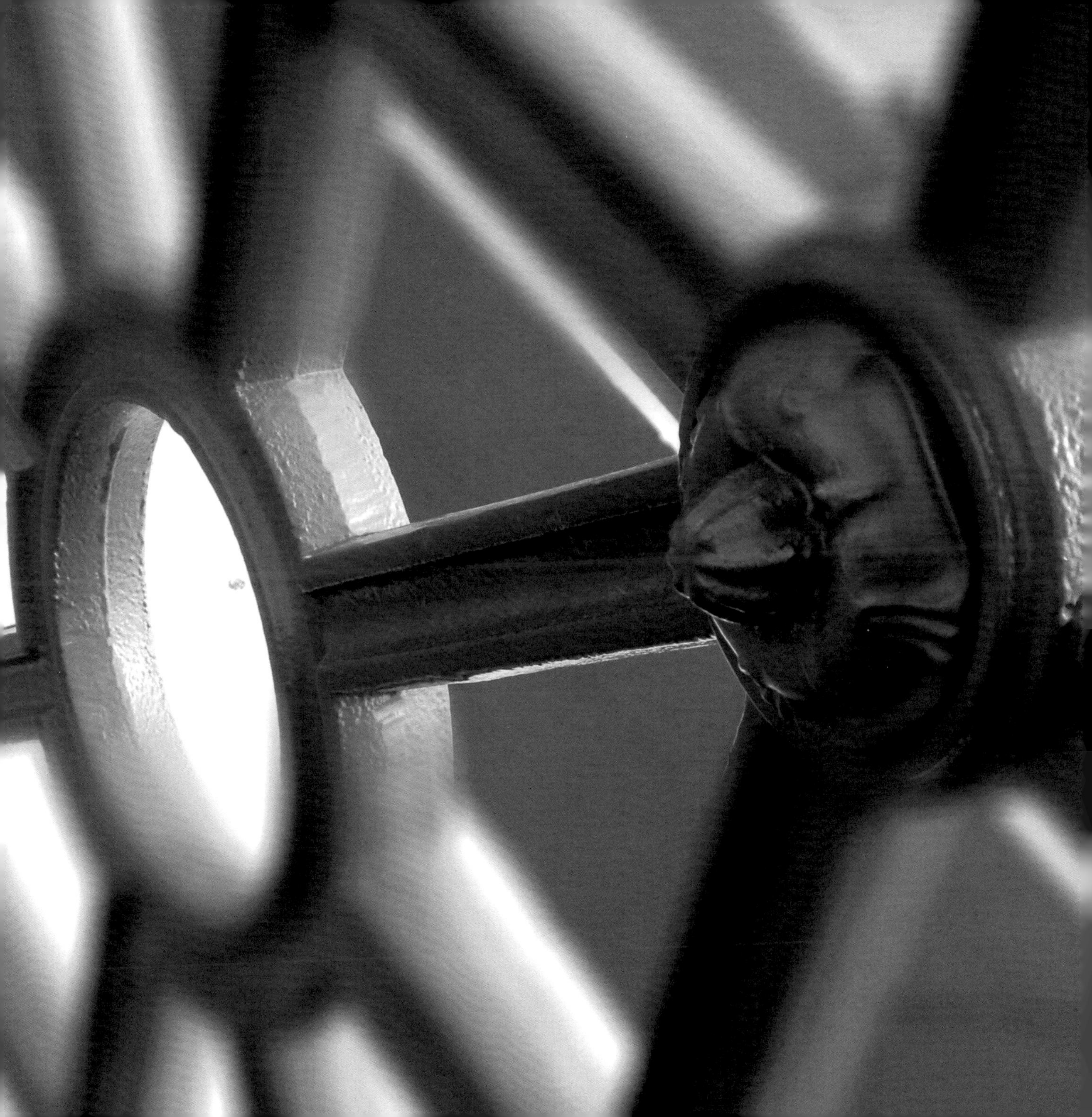

IMAGES OF THE CITY

Photo no. 20: "The Beauty of Iron"

by Veronika Bernard

Budapest, 2013

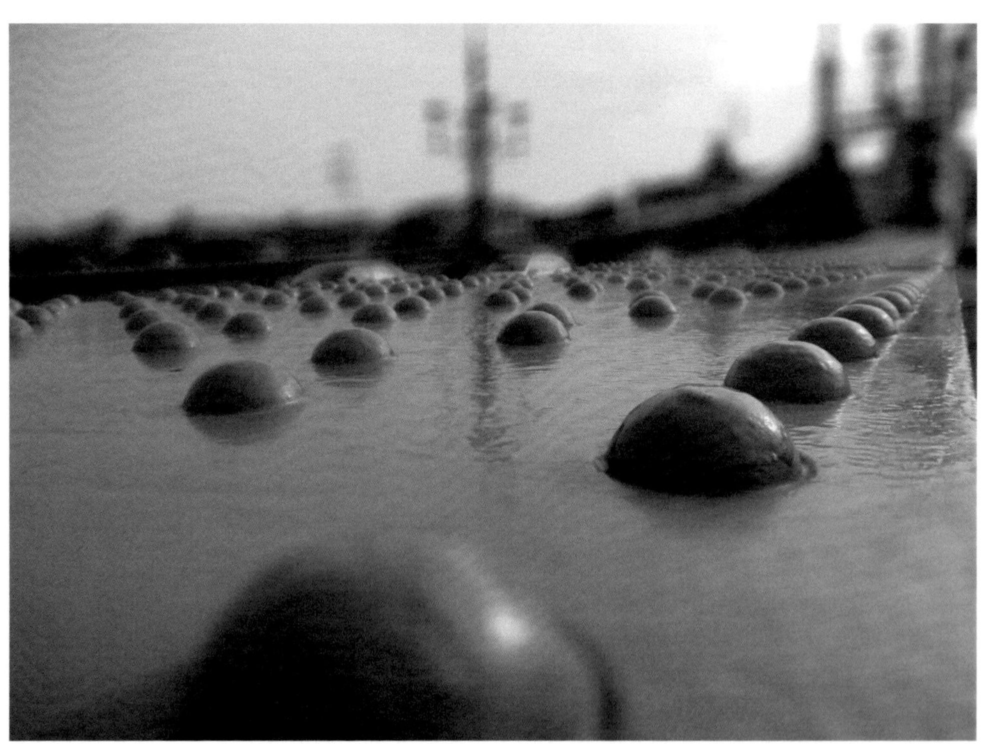

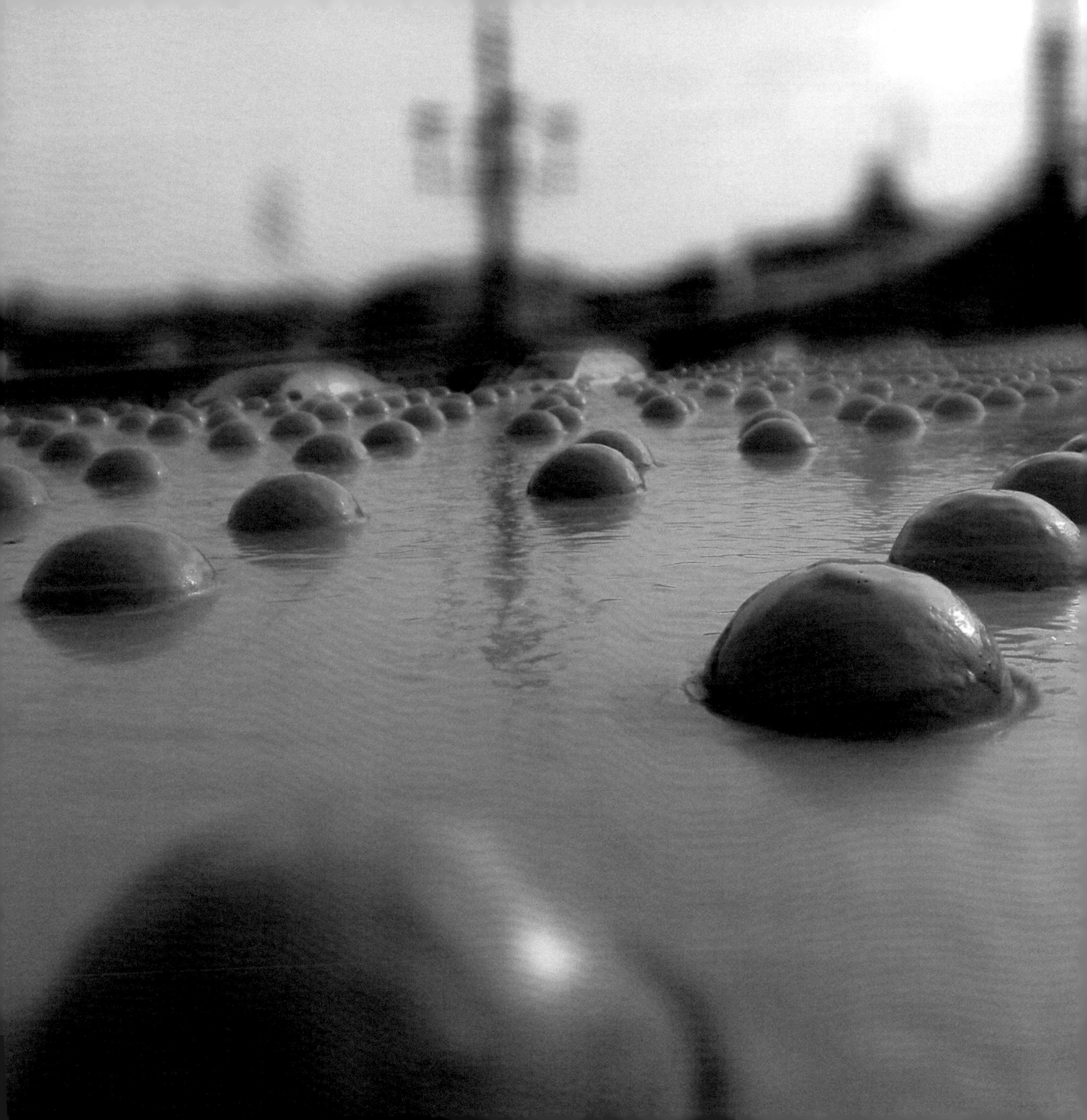

Urban Life

Urbanes Leben

IMAGES OF THE CITY

Photo no. 21: "Counterpoints no. 27"

by Veronika Bernard

Cologne, 2011

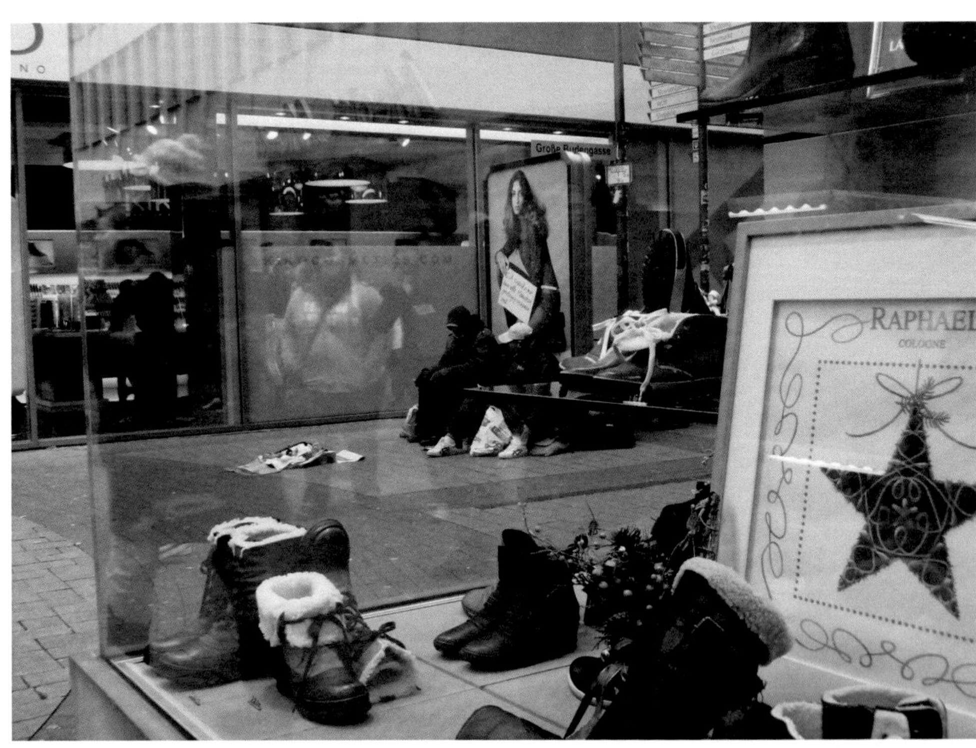

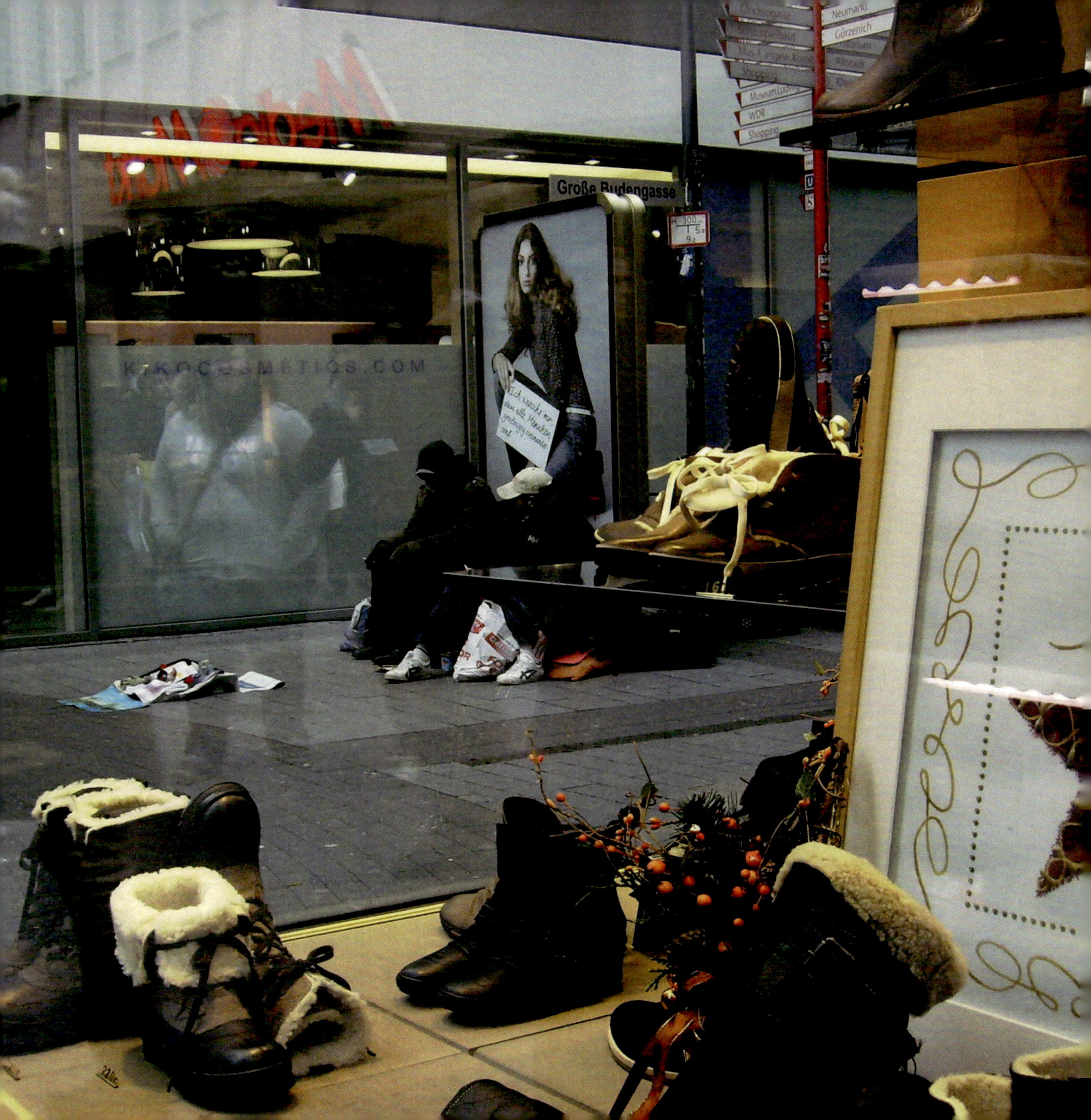
Neumarkt
Gürzenich
WDR
Shopping
Große Budengasse
KIKOCOSMETICS.COM

IMAGES OF THE CITY

Photo no. 22: "Sea of Men & Colours"

by Veronika Bernard

Istanbul, 2007

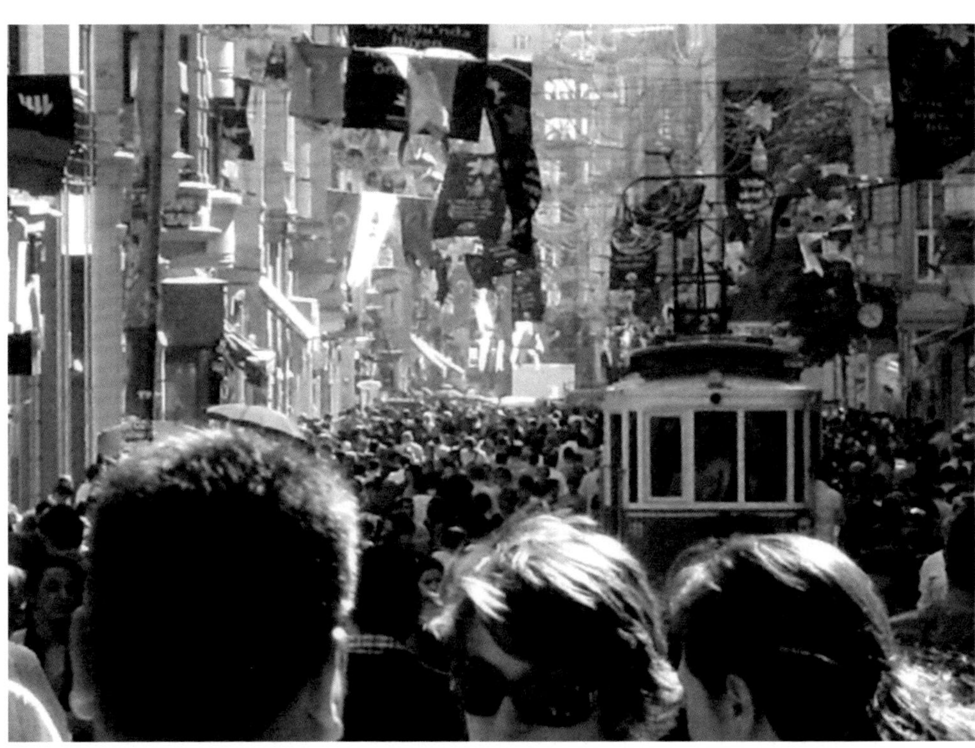

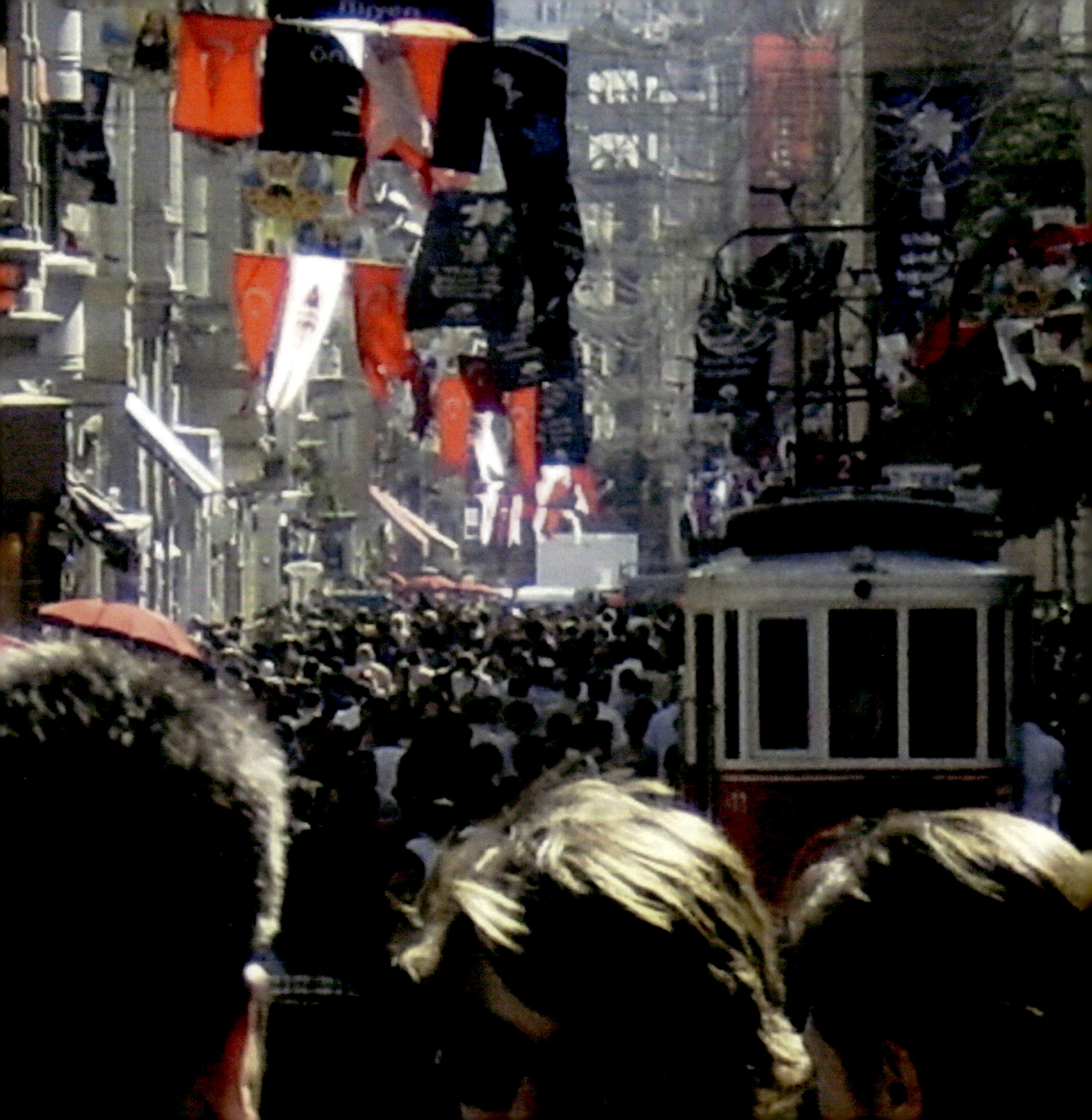

IMAGES OF THE CITY

Photo no. 23: "Counterpoints no. 30"

by Veronika Bernard

Cologne, 2011

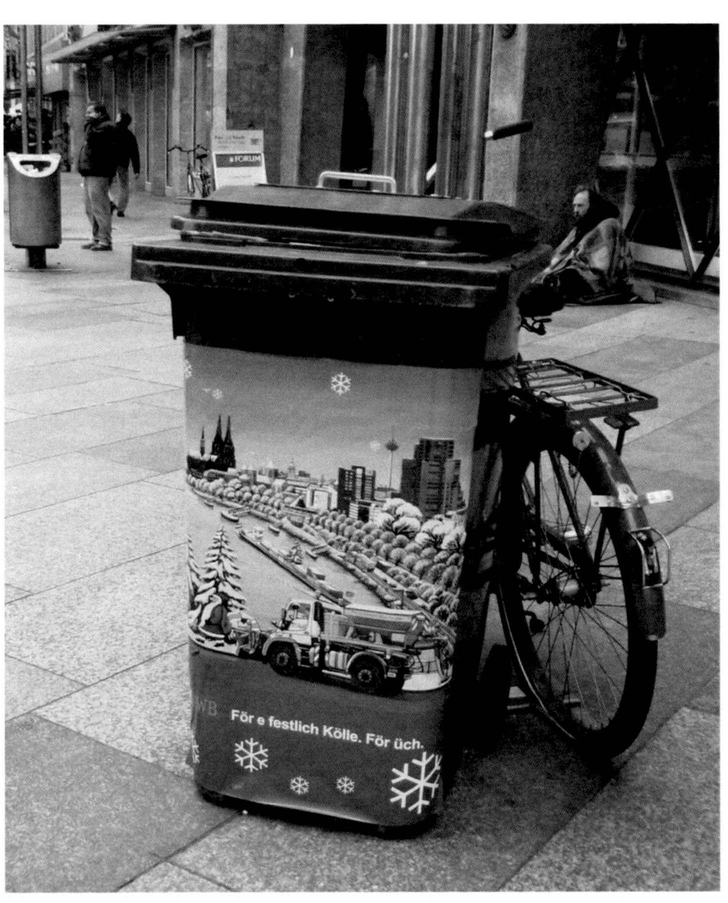

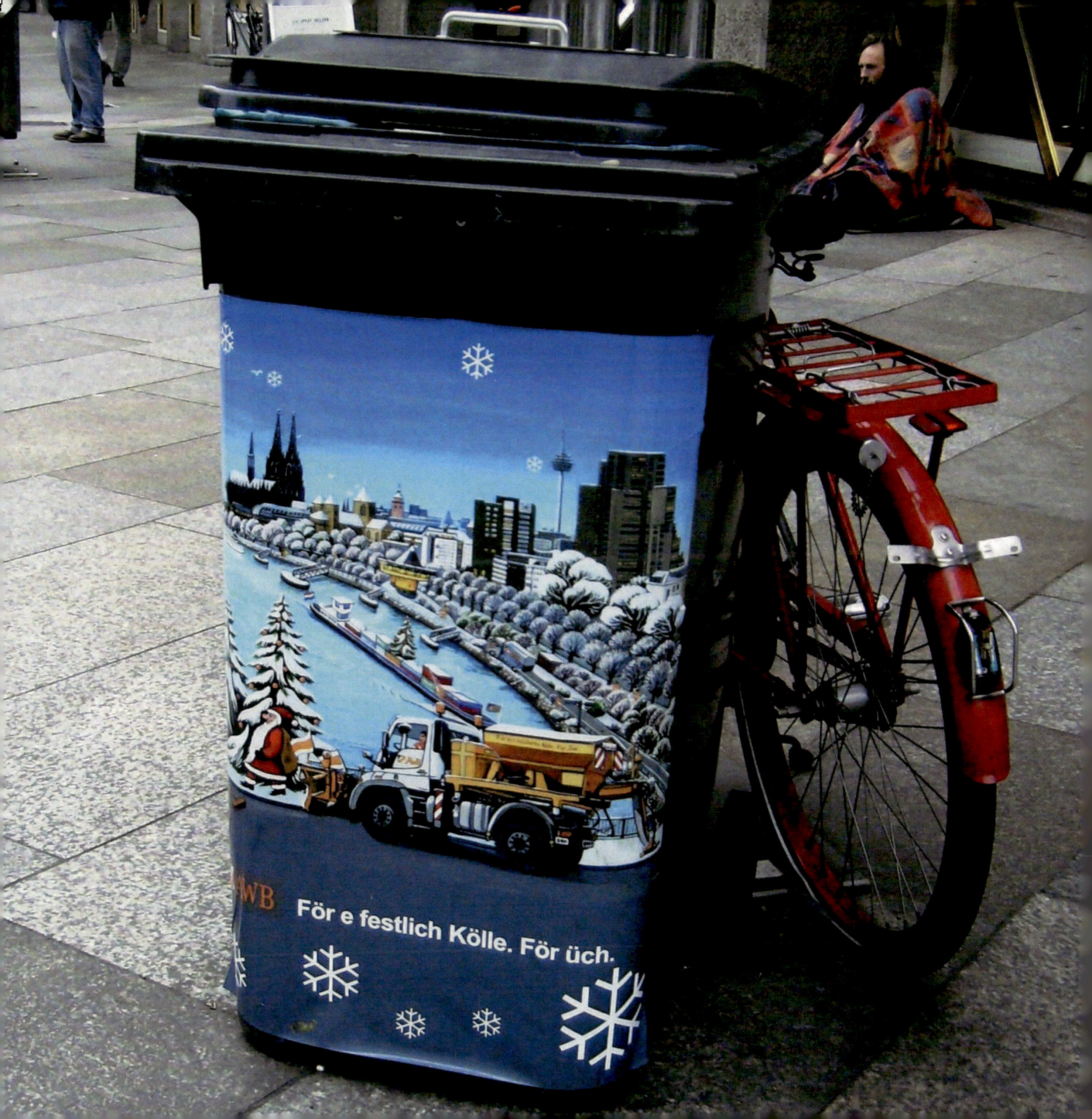
För e festlich Kölle. För üch.

IMAGES OF THE CITY

Photo no. 24: "Life on the River"

by Veronika Bernard

Basel, 2012

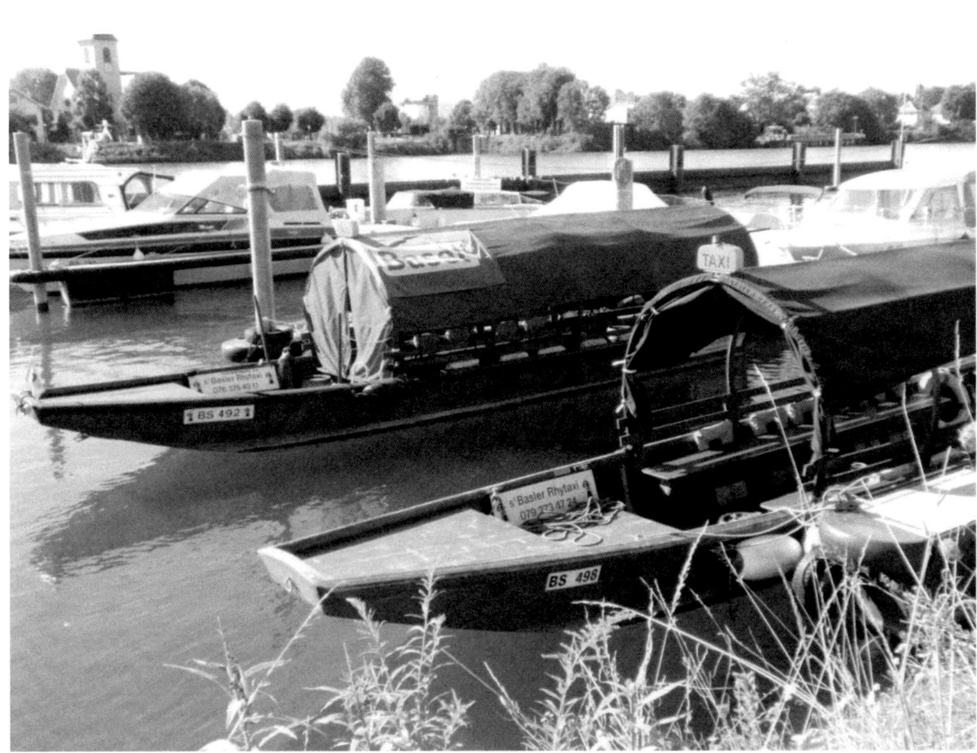

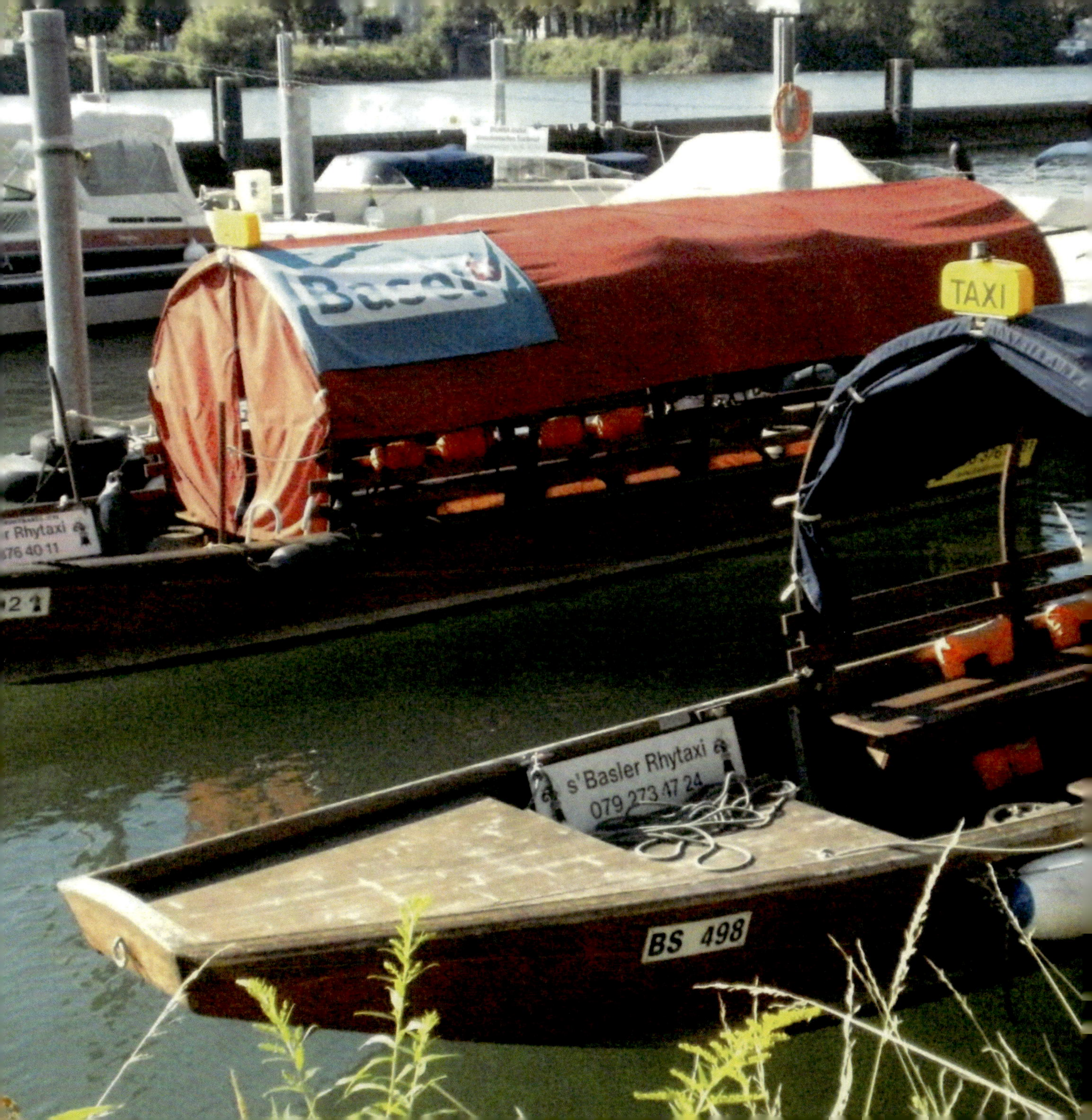
TAXI
s'Basler Rhytaxi
079 273 47 24
BS 498

IMAGES OF THE CITY

Photo no. 25: "From above no. 1"

by Veronika Bernard

Istanbul, 2012

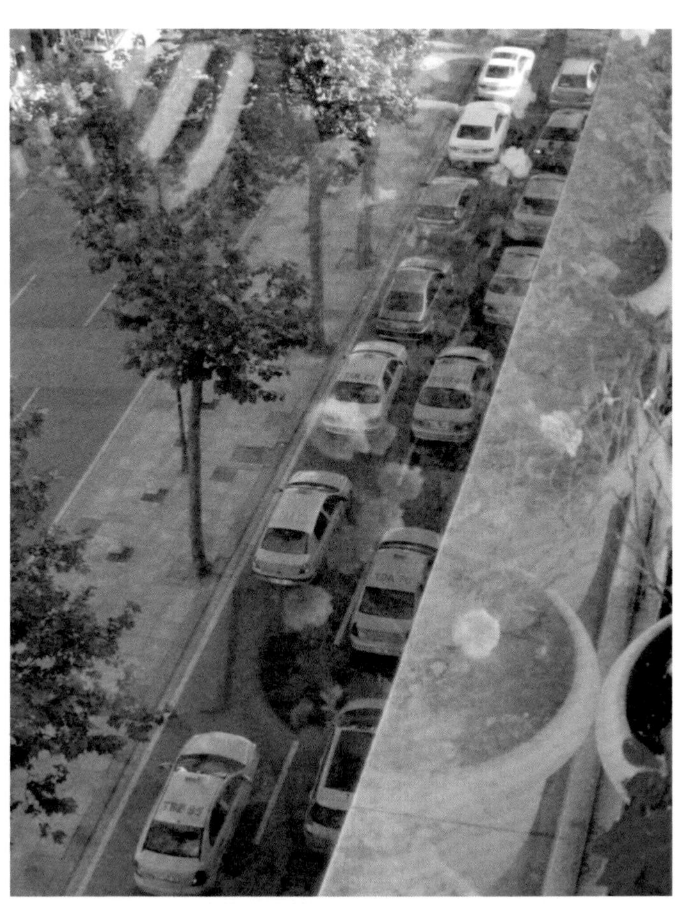

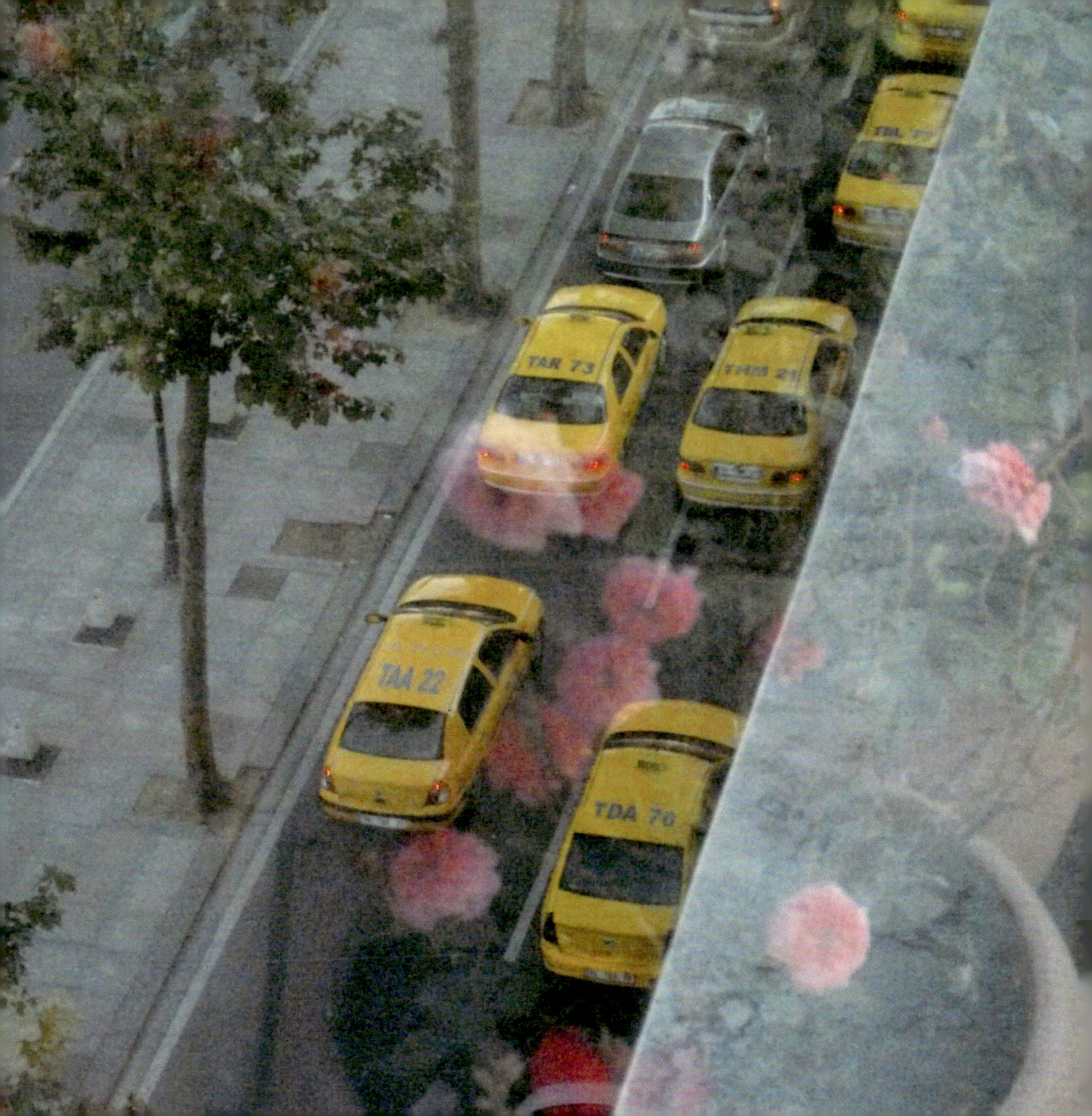
TAR 73
TAA 22
TDA 70

IMAGES OF THE CITY

Photo no. 26: "Worlds"

by Veronika Bernard

Cologne, 2013

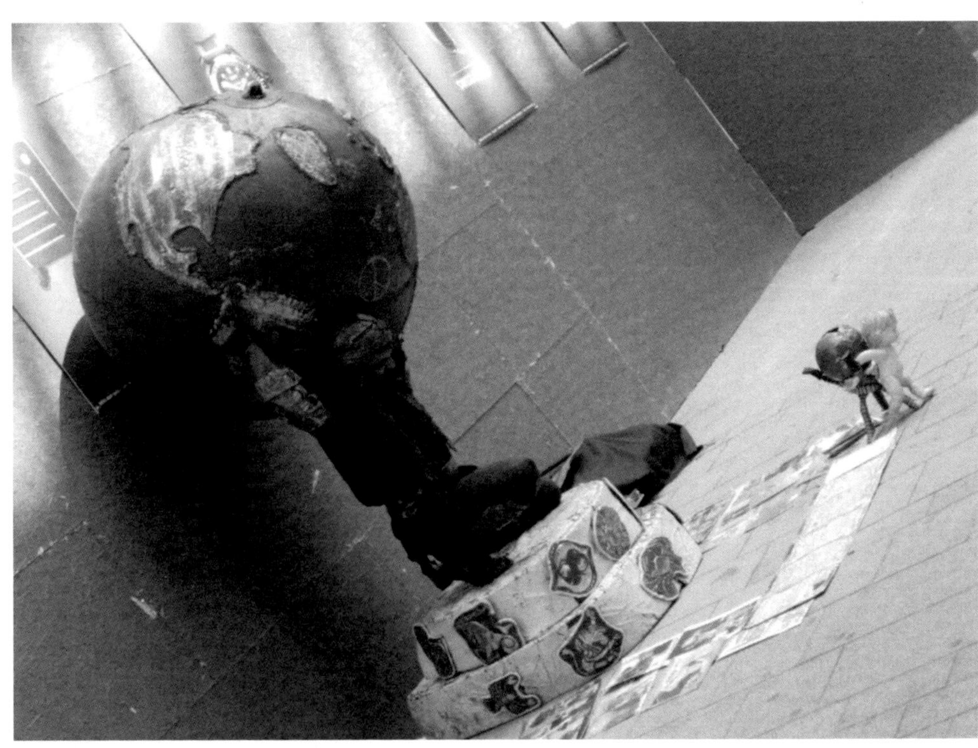

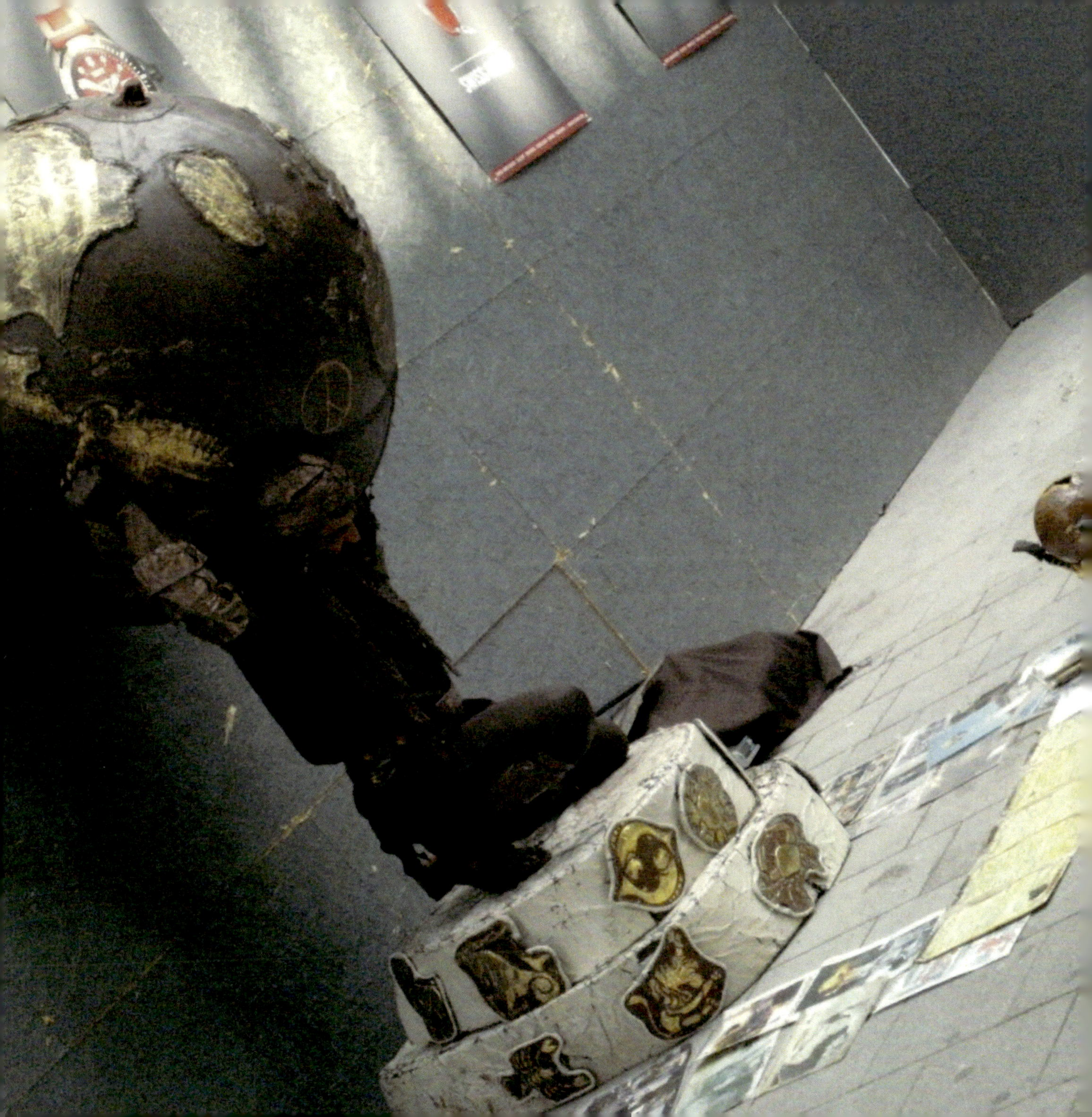

IMAGES OF THE CITY

Photo no. 27: "It's a Bright Life no. 1"

by Veronika Bernard

Bratislava, 2013

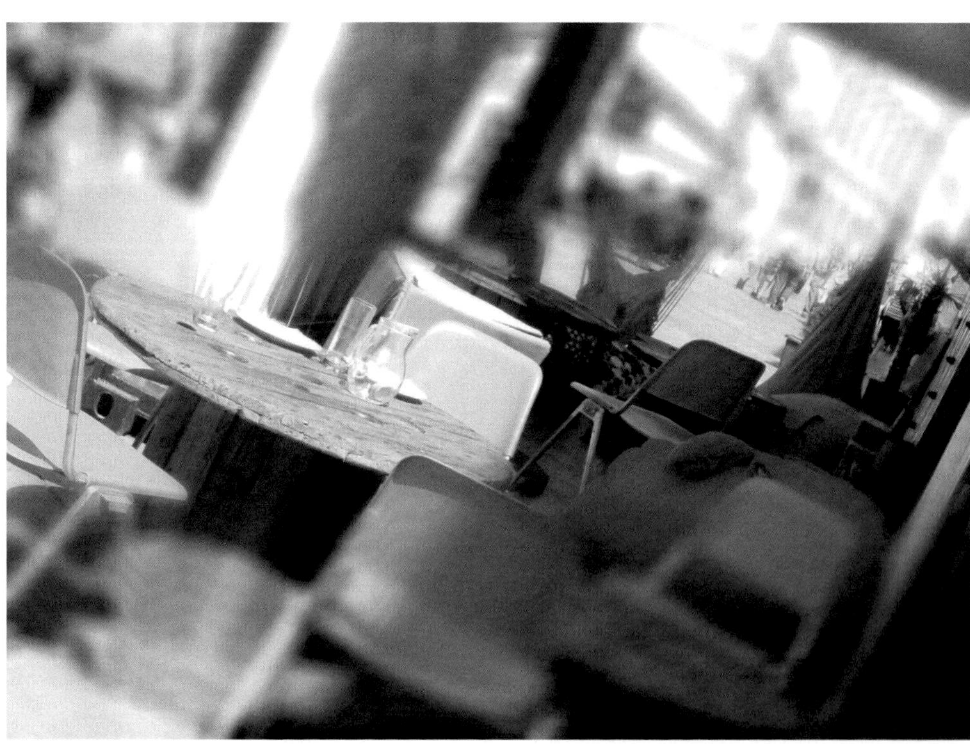

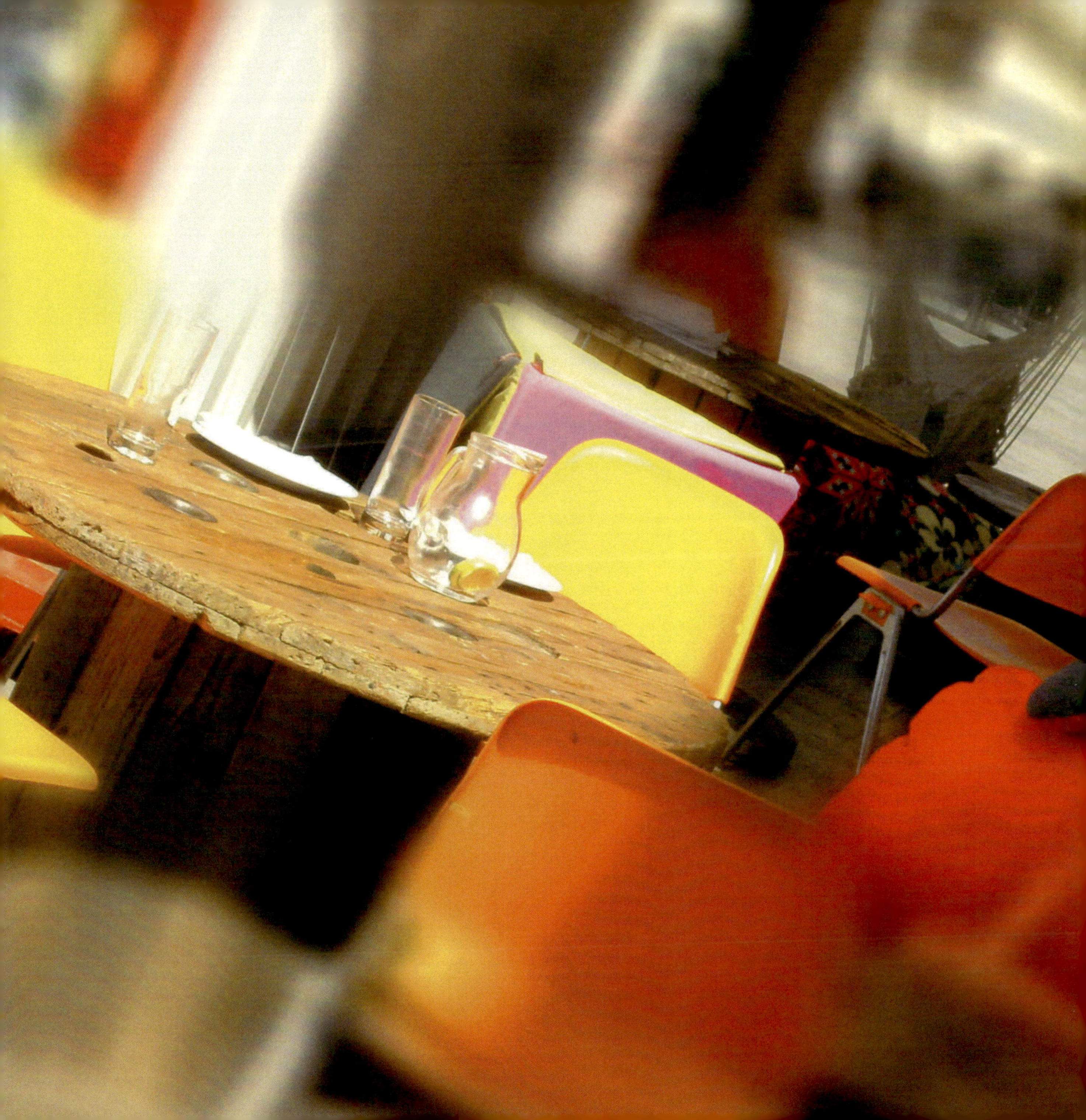

IMAGES OF THE CITY

Photo no. 28: "Copied Life"

by Veronika Bernard

Bratislava, 2013

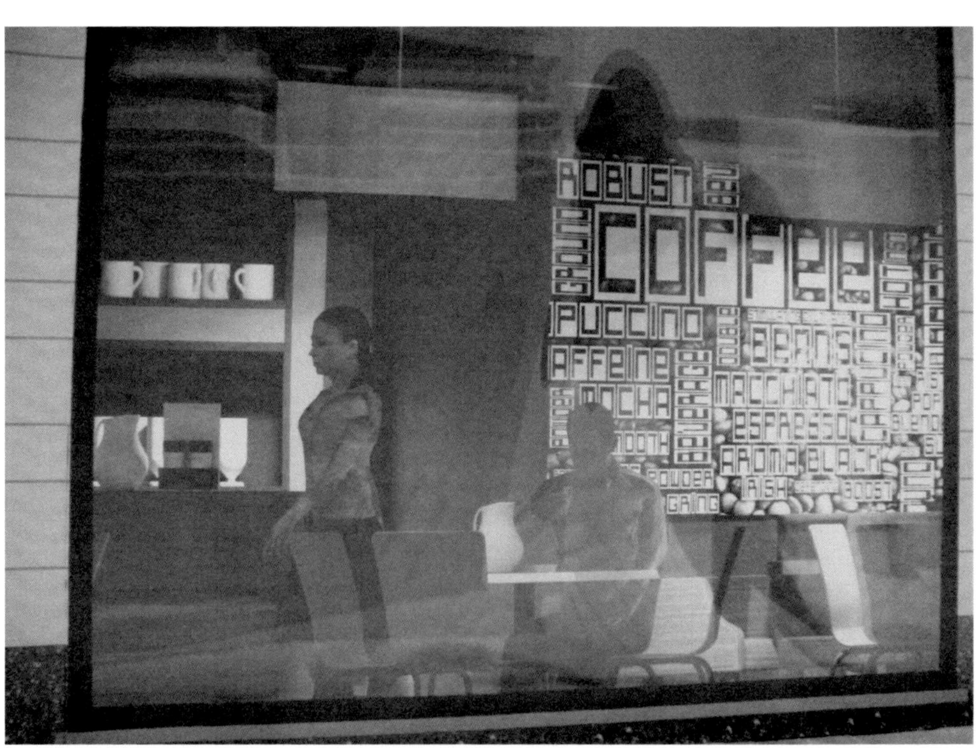

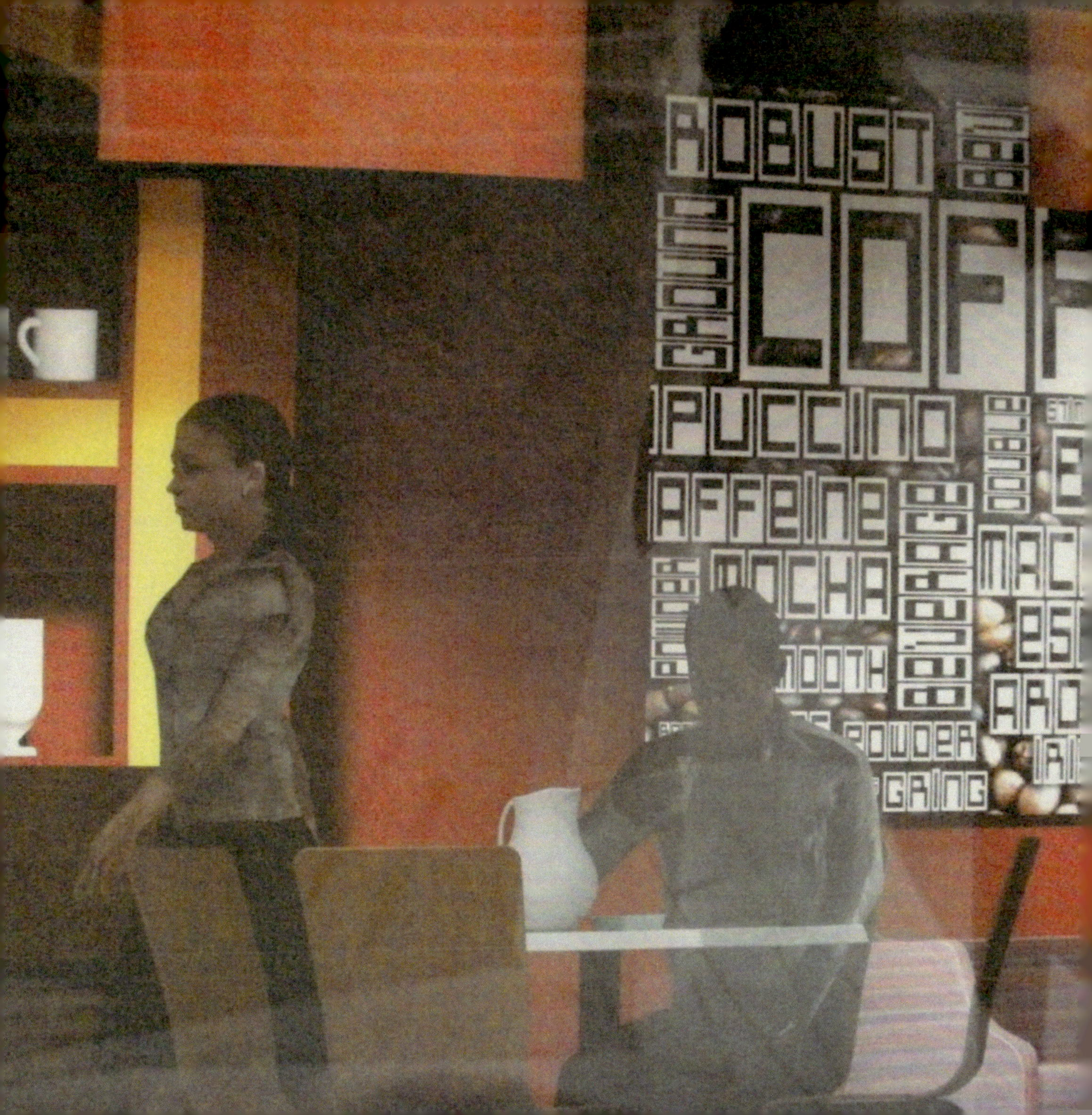
ROBUST
MOCHA
POWDER

IMAGES OF THE CITY

Photo no. 29: "Urban Lights"

by Veronika Bernard

Berlin, 2012

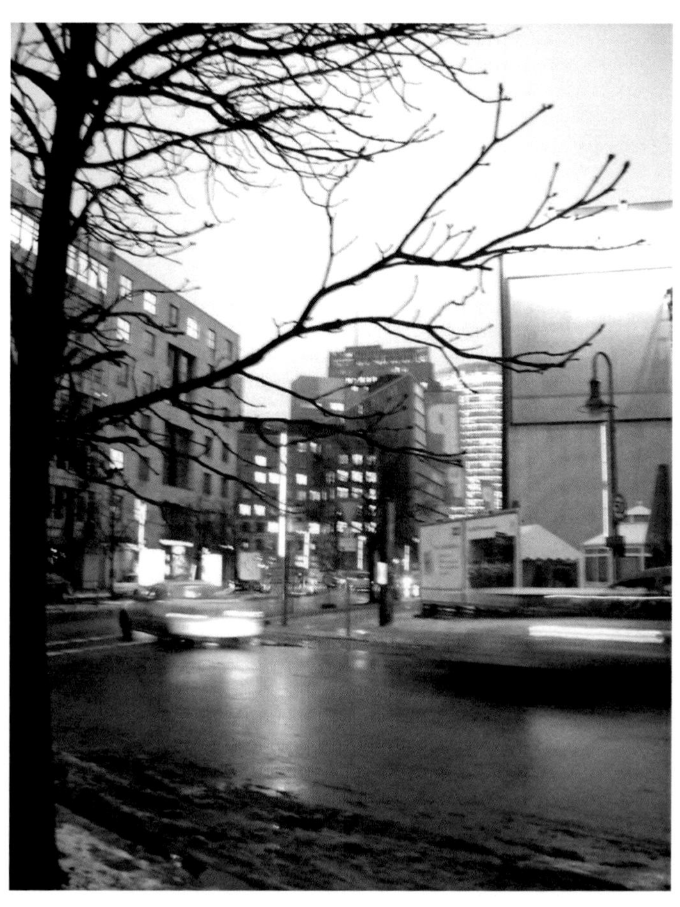

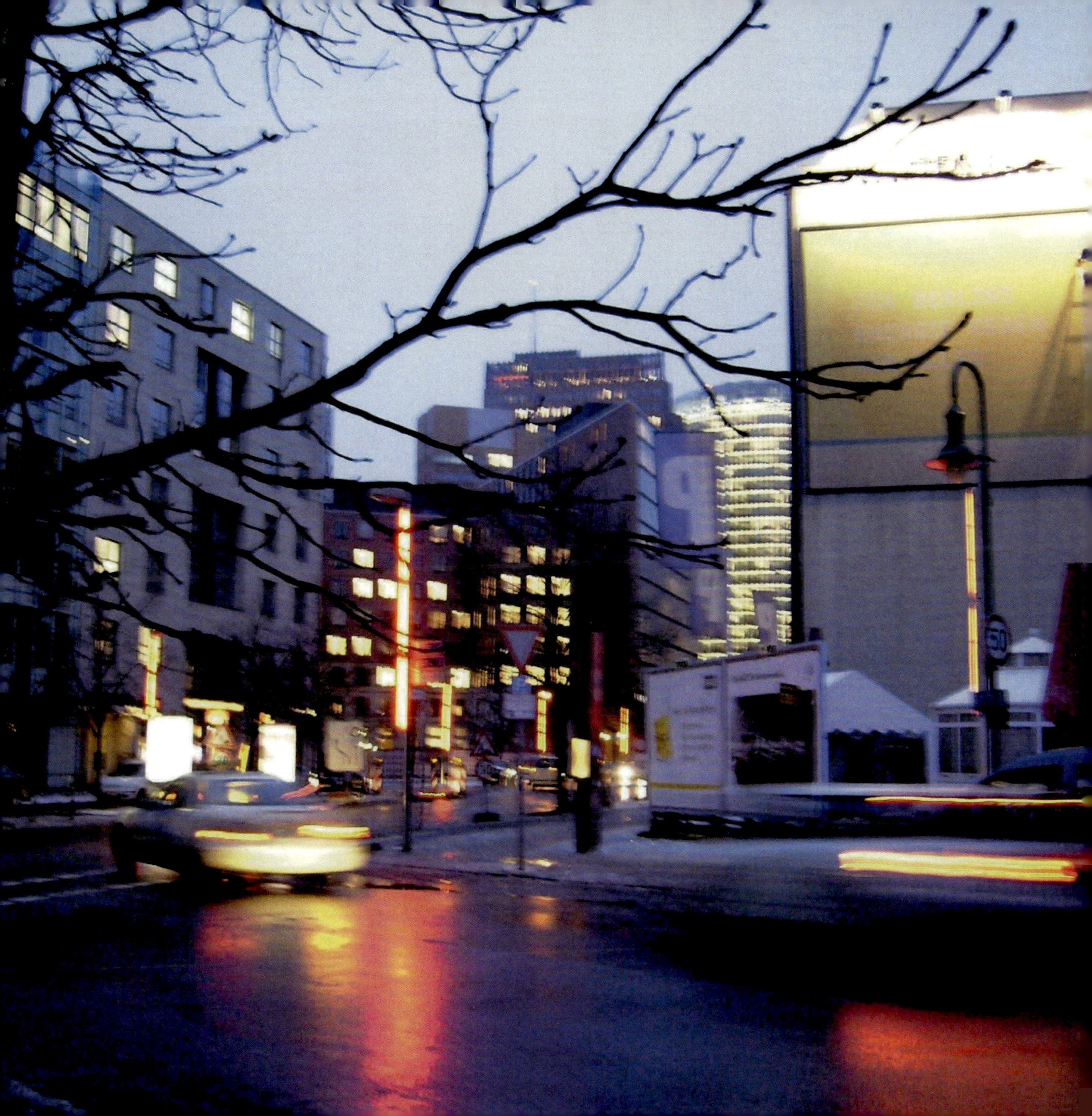
50

IMAGES OF THE CITY

Photo no. 30: "Keeping the Landmark"

by Veronika Bernard

Cologne, 2008

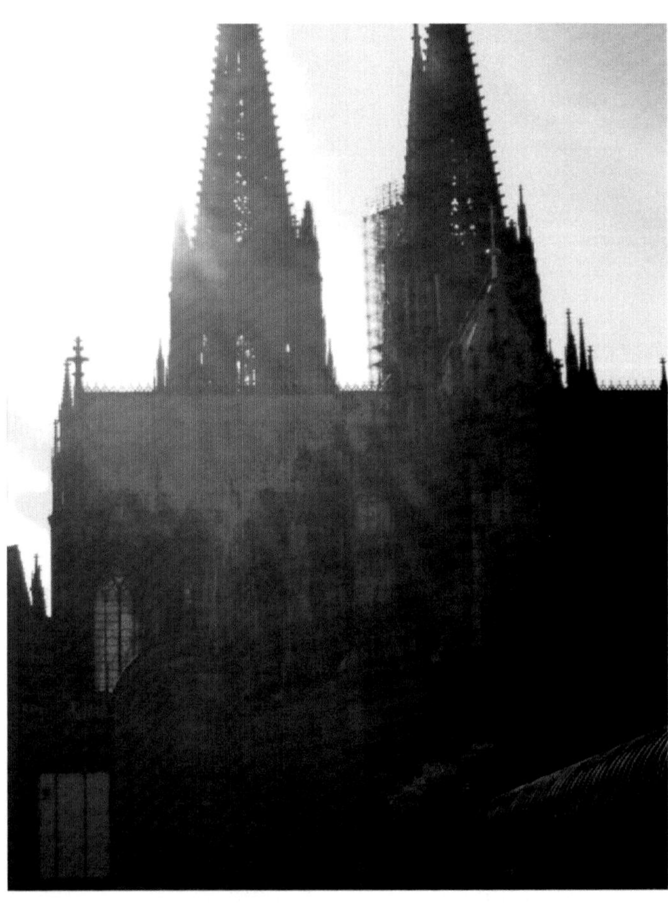

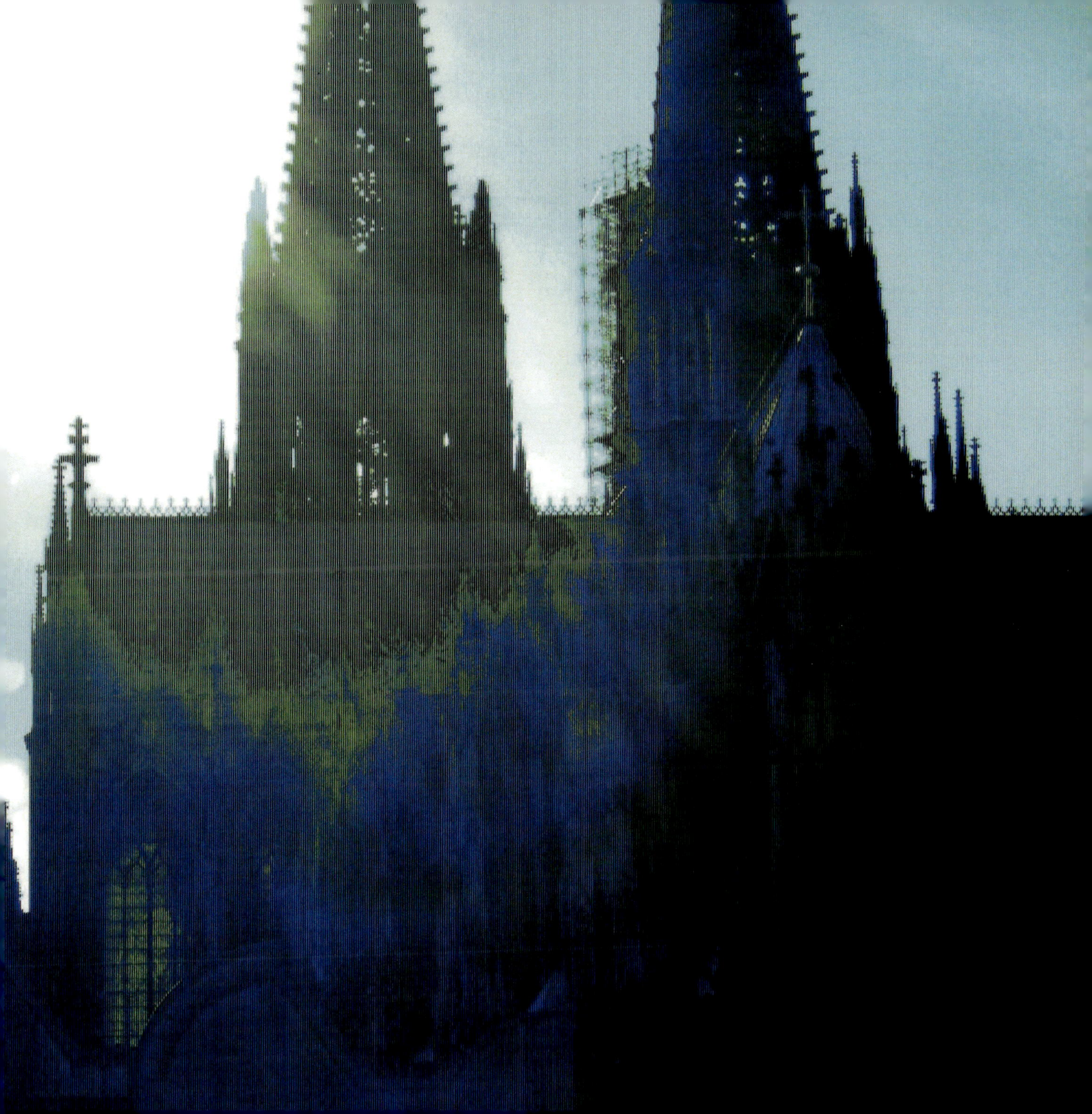

IMAGES OF THE CITY

Photo no. 30: "It's a Commercial World"

by Veronika Bernard

Berlin (Potsdamer Platz), 2012

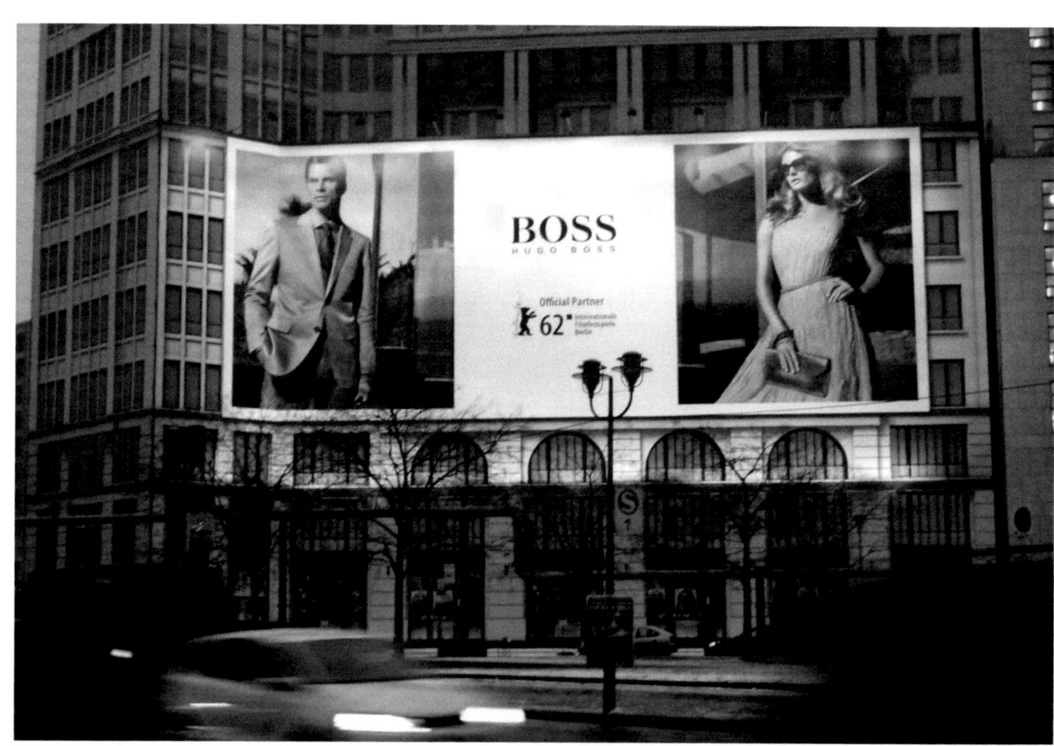

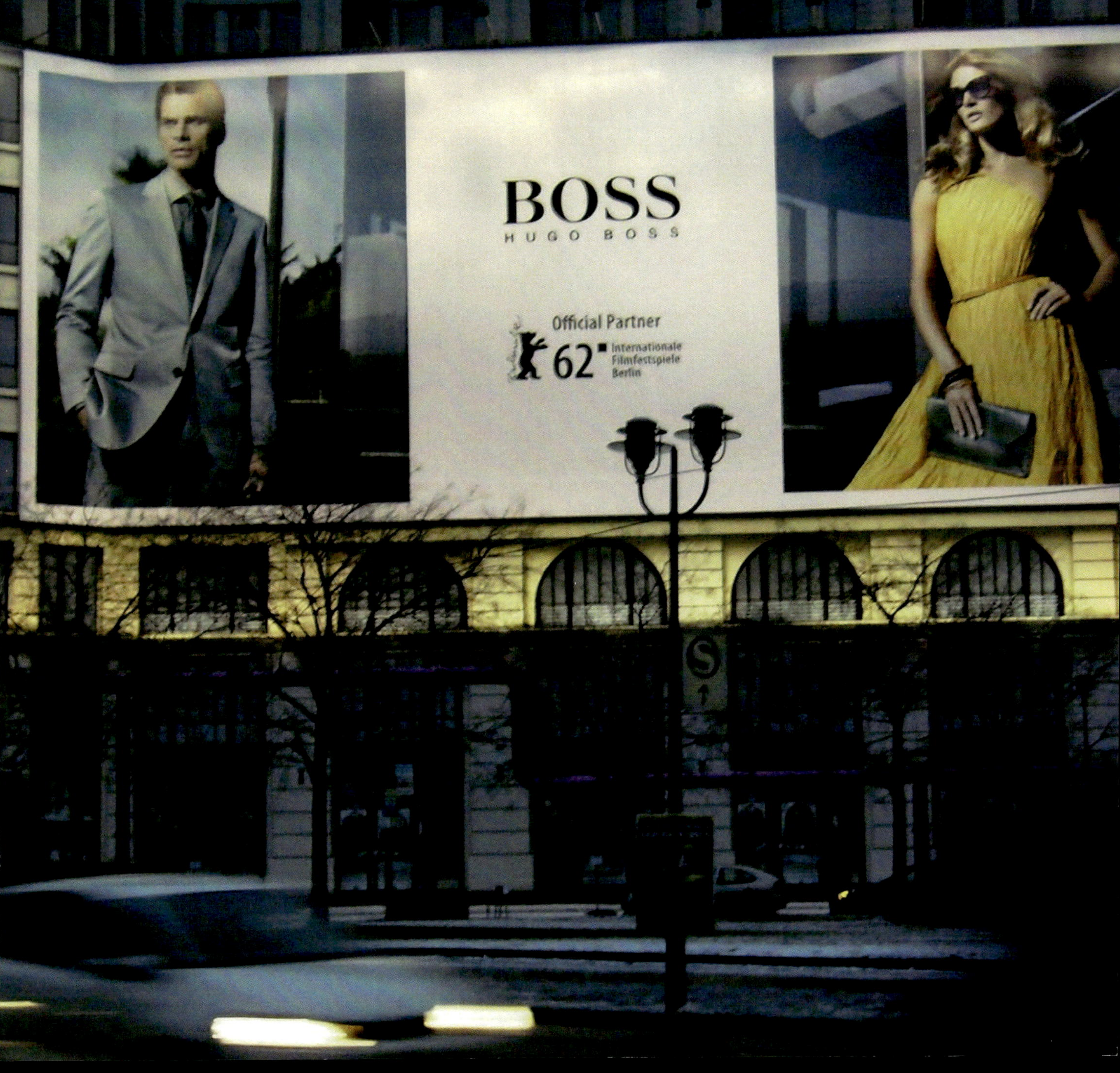
BOSS
HUGO BOSS
Official Partner
62.
Internationale
Filmfestspiele
Berlin
S

IMAGES OF THE CITY

Photo no. 31: "Kitten Shooting"

by Veronika Bernard

Istanbul, 2009

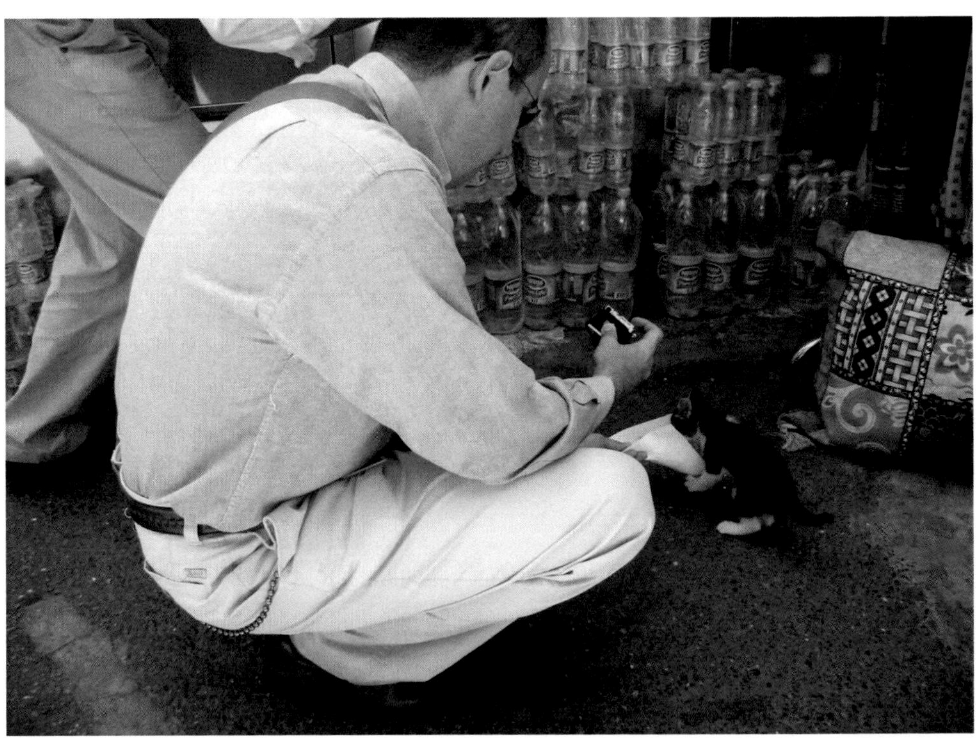

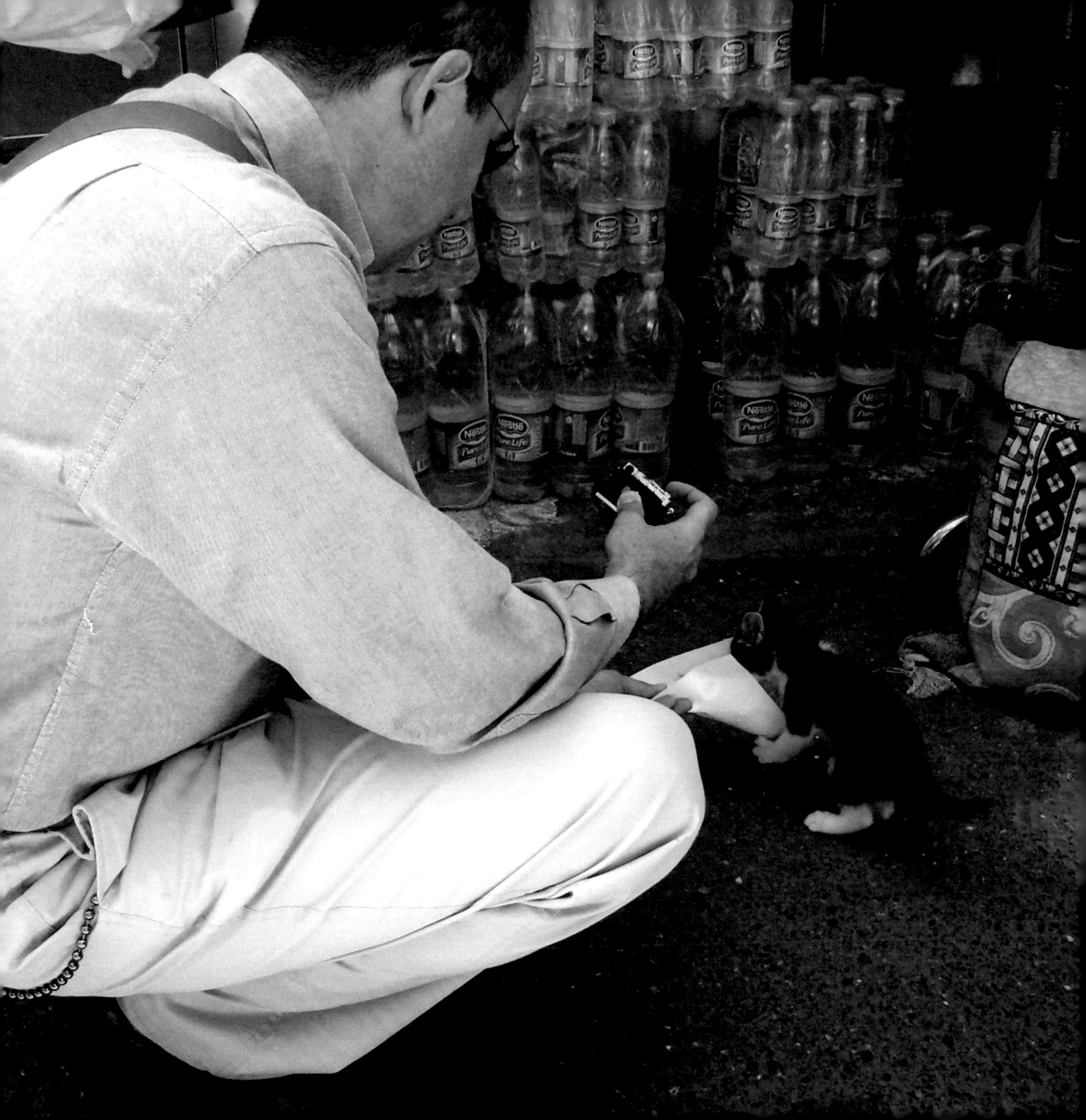
Nestlé
Pure Life

IMAGES OF THE CITY

Photo no. 31: "Counterpoints no. 31"

by Veronika Bernard

Berlin, 2012

MOTEL ONE
Entdecken Sie
eine neue
Einkaufsdimension!

IMAGES OF THE CITY

Photo no. 32: "Industrial"

by Veronika Bernard

Basel, 2012

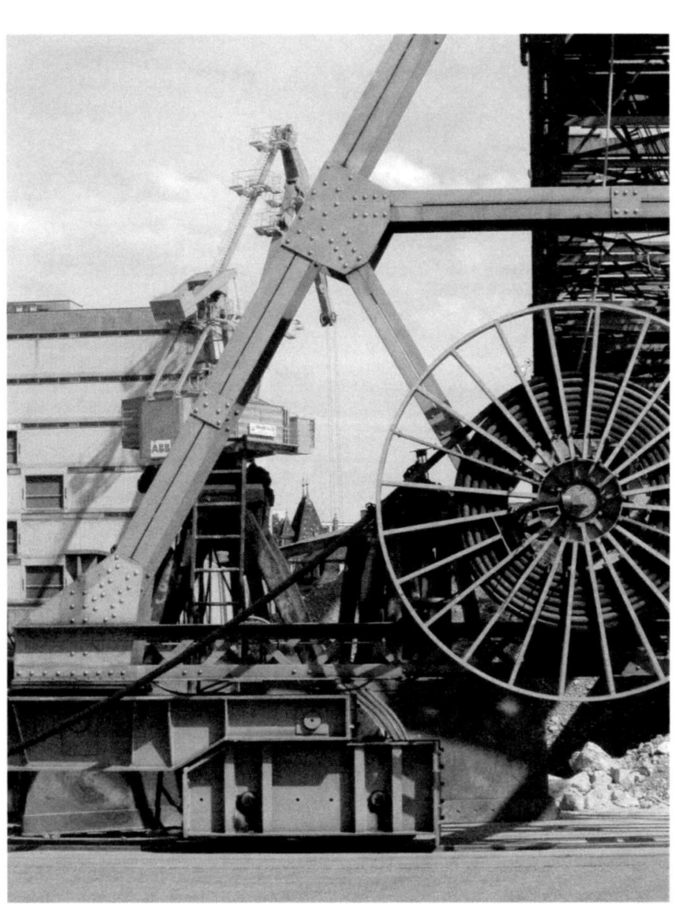

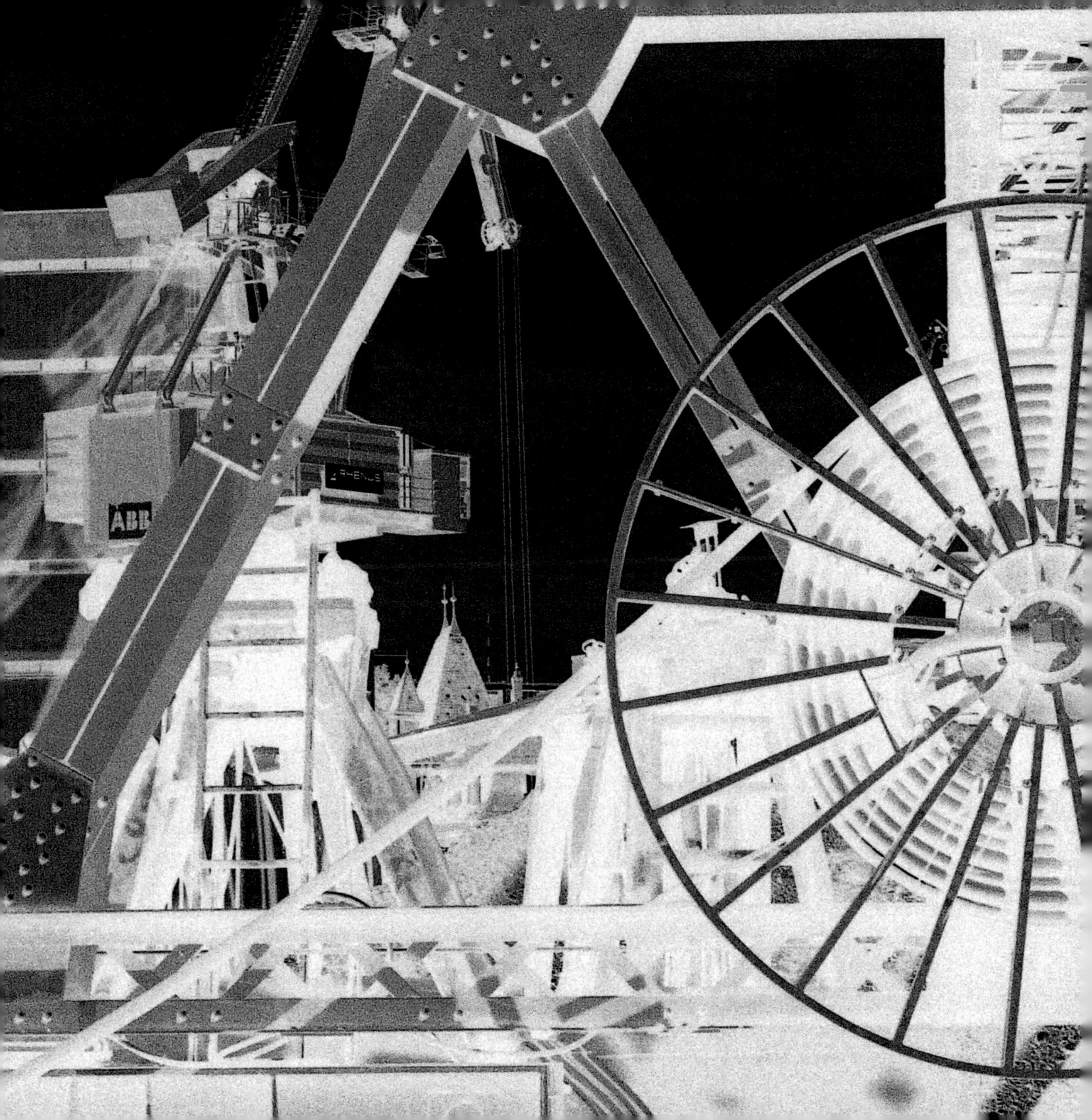
ABB
RHENUS

IMAGES OF THE CITY

Photo no. 33: "Lovely Monster"

by Veronika Bernard

Lyon, 2011

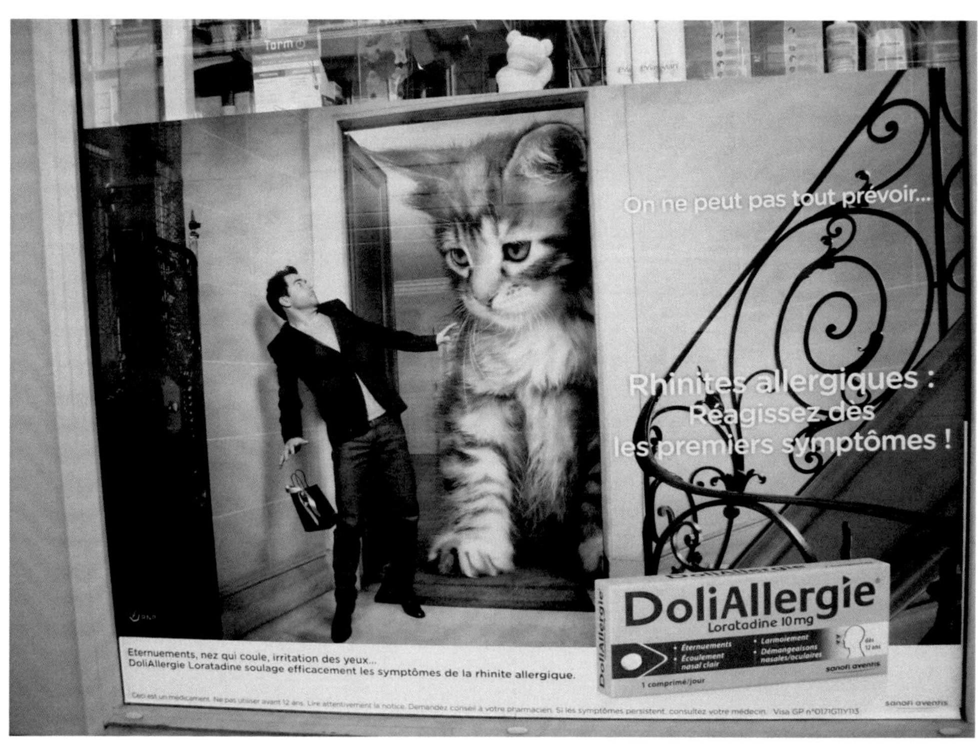

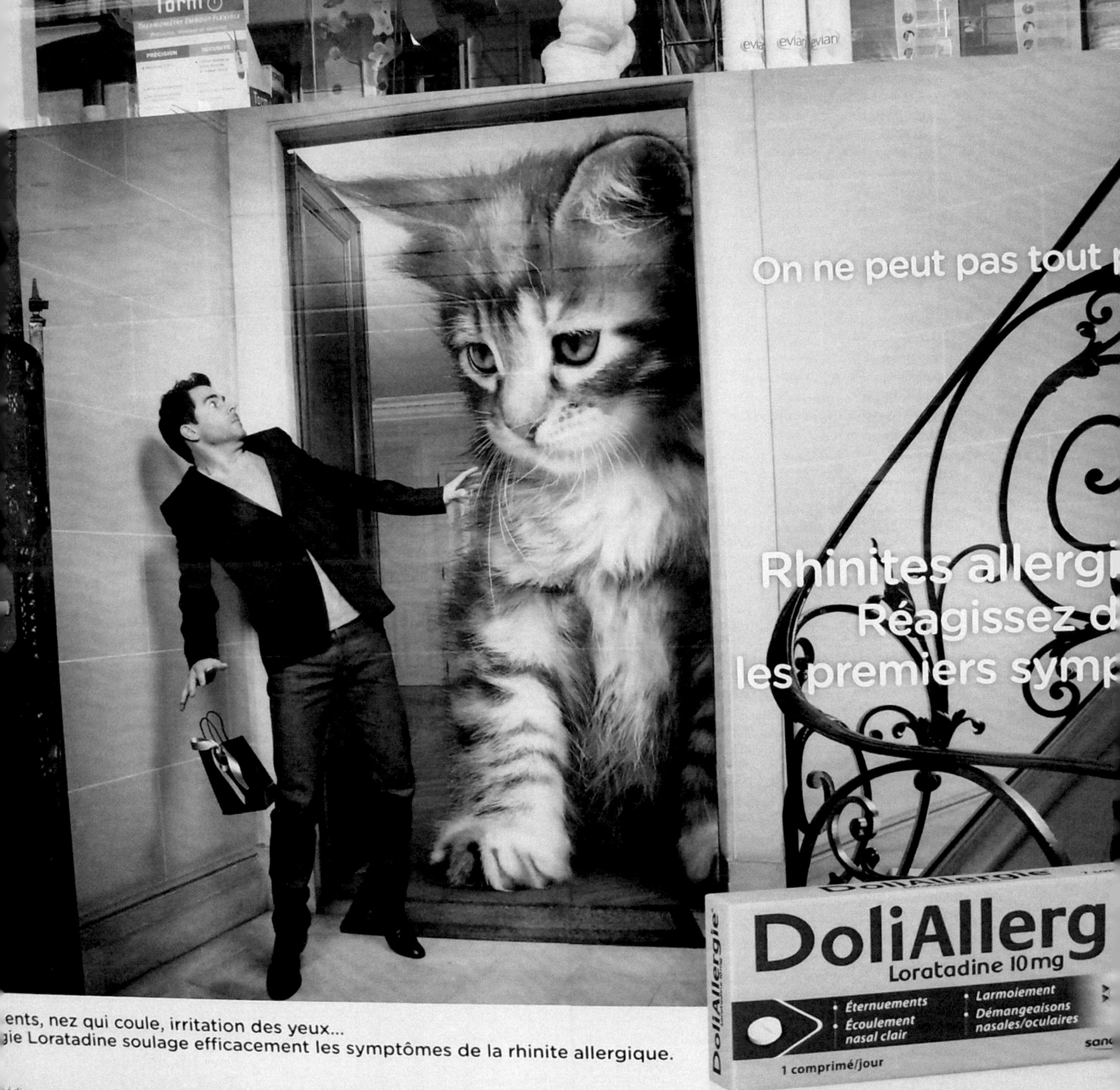
Torm
evian
On ne peut pas tout p
Rhinites allergi
Réagissez d
les premiers symp
ents, nez qui coule, irritation des yeux...
gie Loratadine soulage efficacement les symptômes de la rhinite allergique.
DoliAllerg
Loratadine 10mg
DoliAllergie
Éternuements
Écoulement nasal clair
Larmoiement
Démangeaisons nasales/oculaires
1 comprimé/jour
édicament. Ne pas utiliser avant 12 ans. Lire attentivement la notice. Demandez conseil à votre pharmacien. Si les symptômes persistent, consultez votre médecin. Visa GP n°0171G1

IMAGES OF THE CITY

Photo no. 34: "Life"

by Veronika Bernard

Avignon, 2011

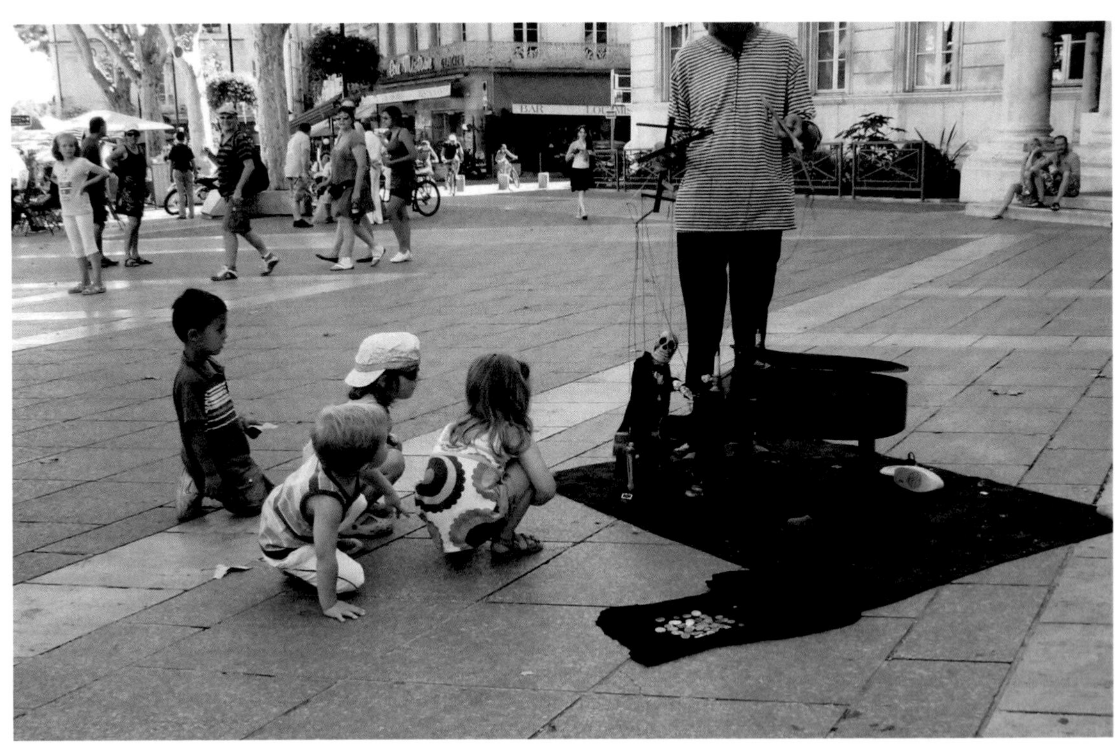

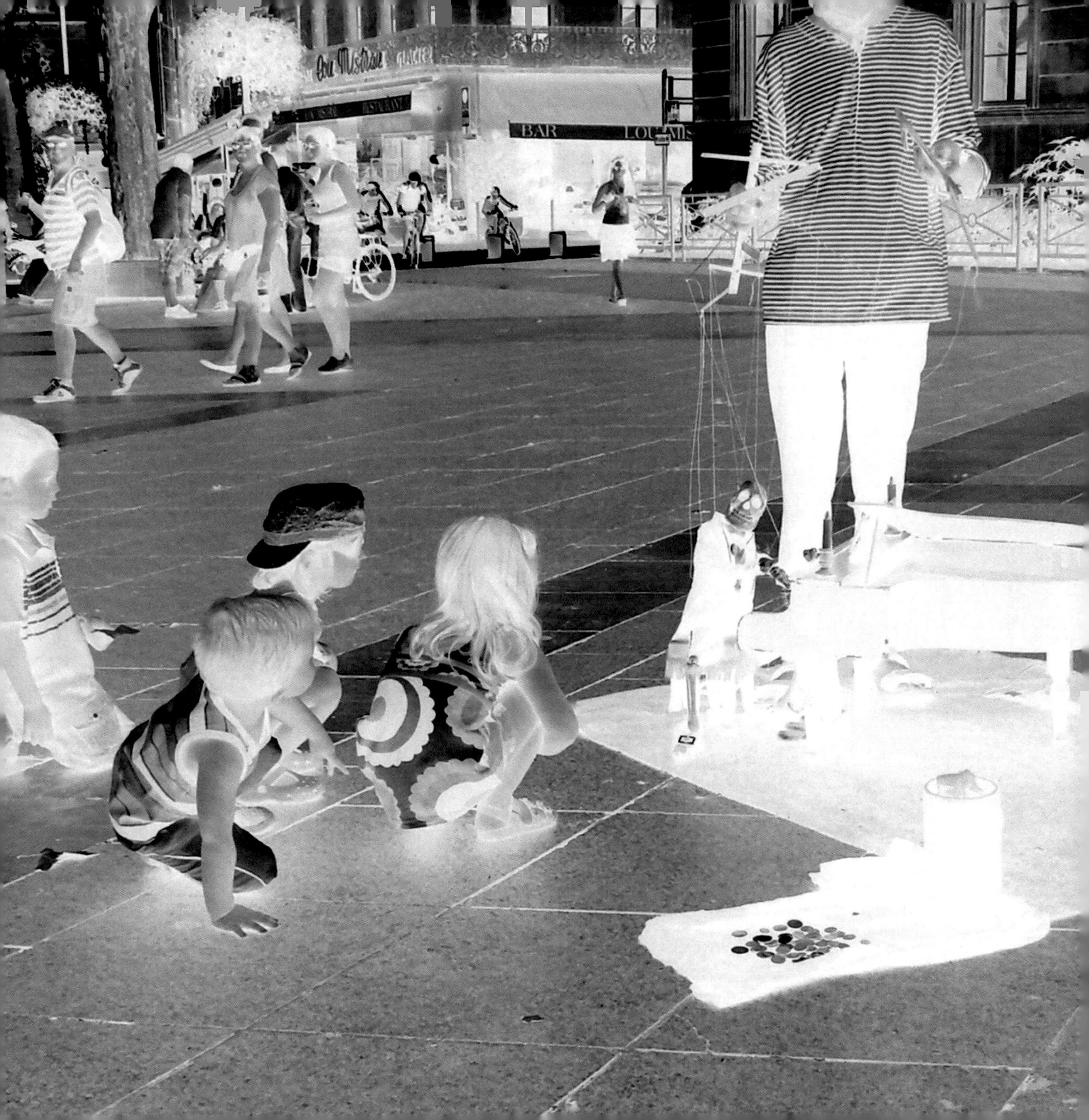
BAR

IMAGES OF THE CITY

Photo no. 35: "Traditional Istanbul"

by Veronika Bernard

Istanbul, 2009

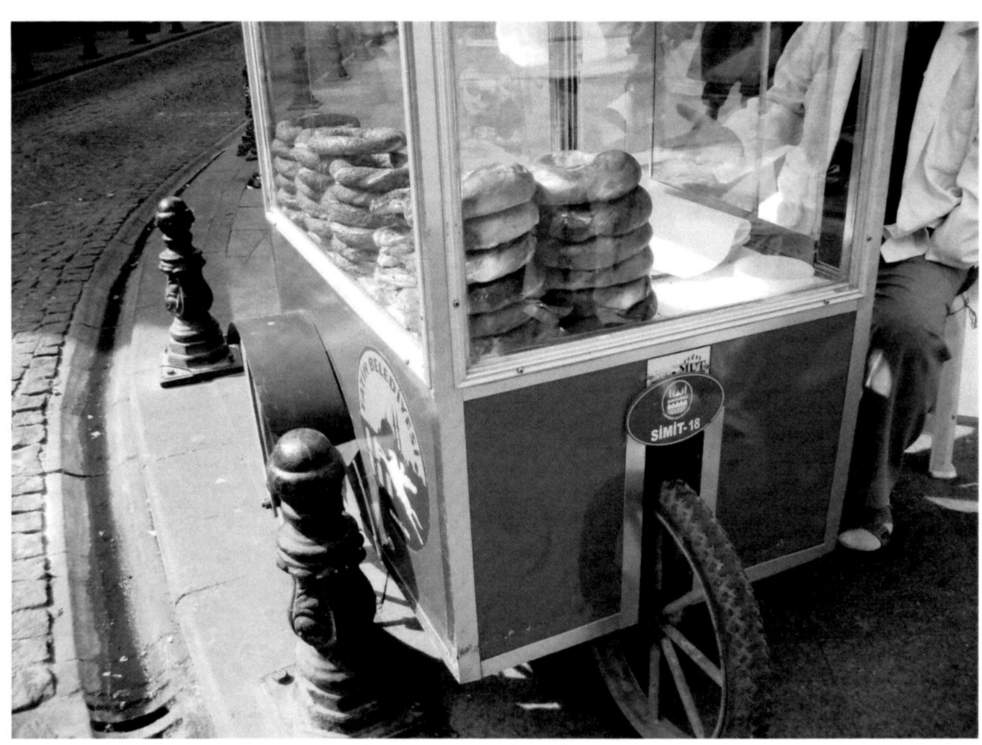

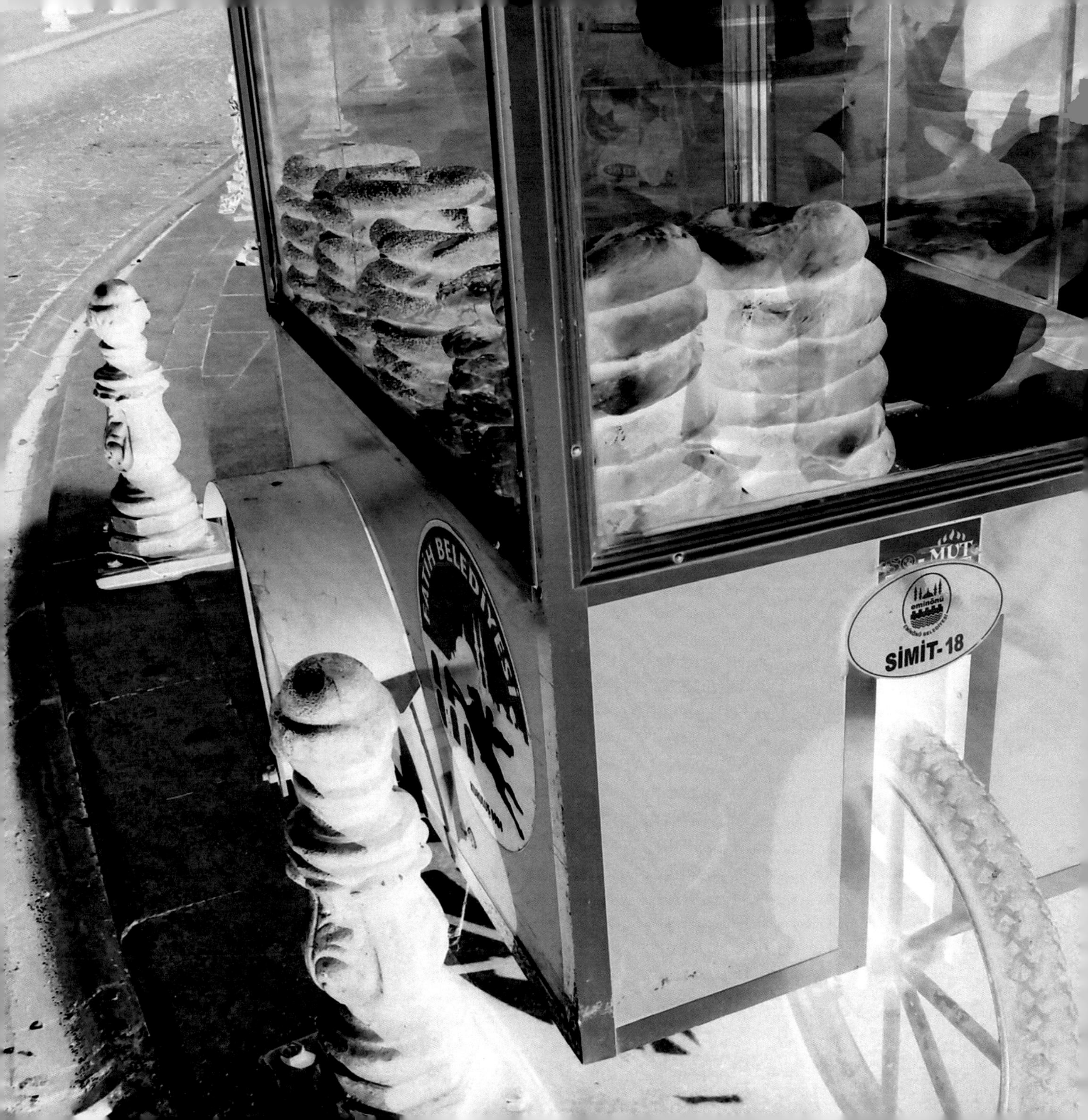
FATİH BELEDİYESİ
eminönü
SİMİT-18

IMAGES OF THE CITY

Photo no. 36: "Urban Veins"

by Veronika Bernard

Basel, 2012

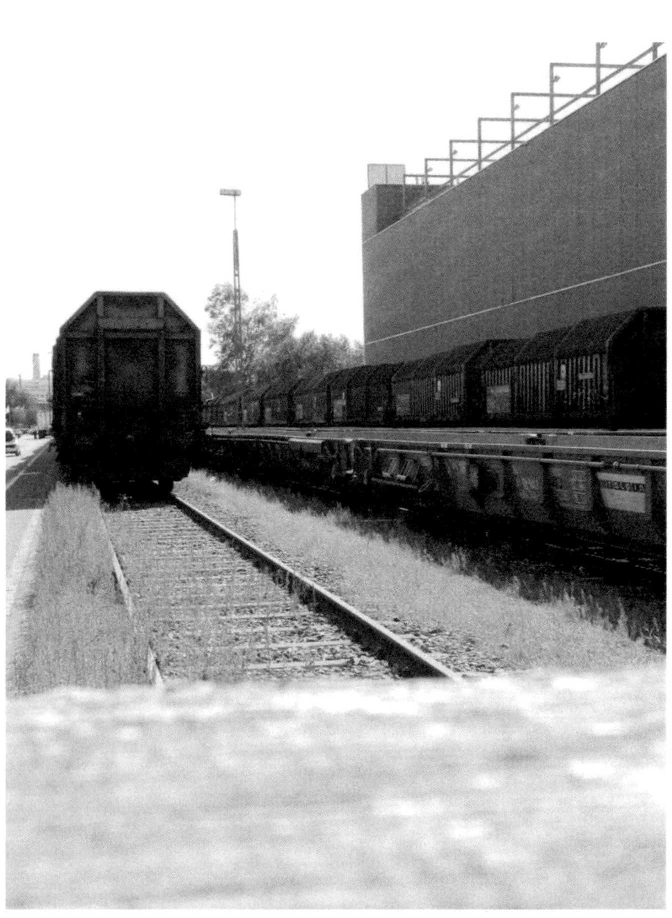

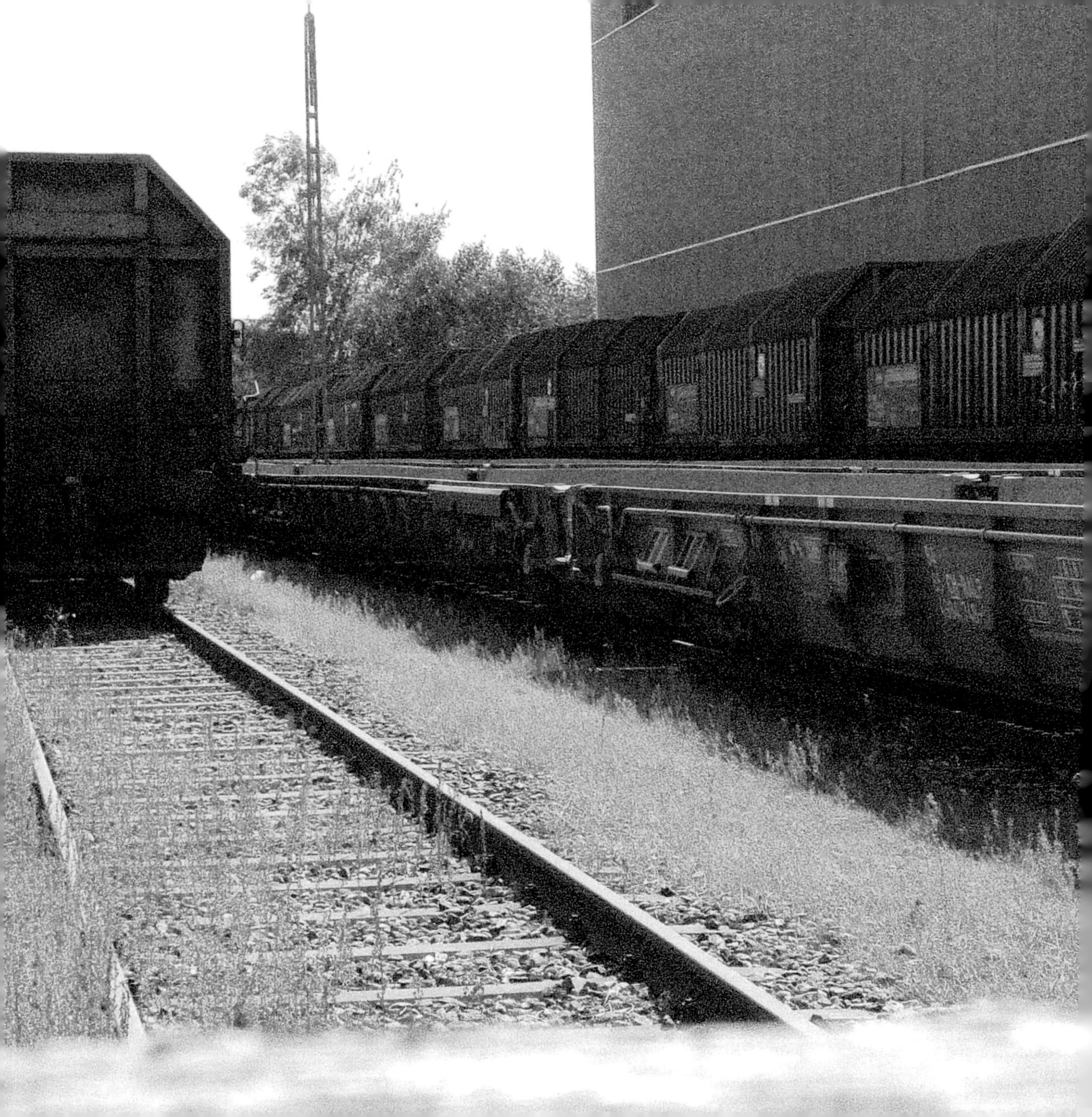

IMAGES OF THE CITY

Photo no. 37: "Artificial"

by Veronika Bernard

Innsbruck, 2012

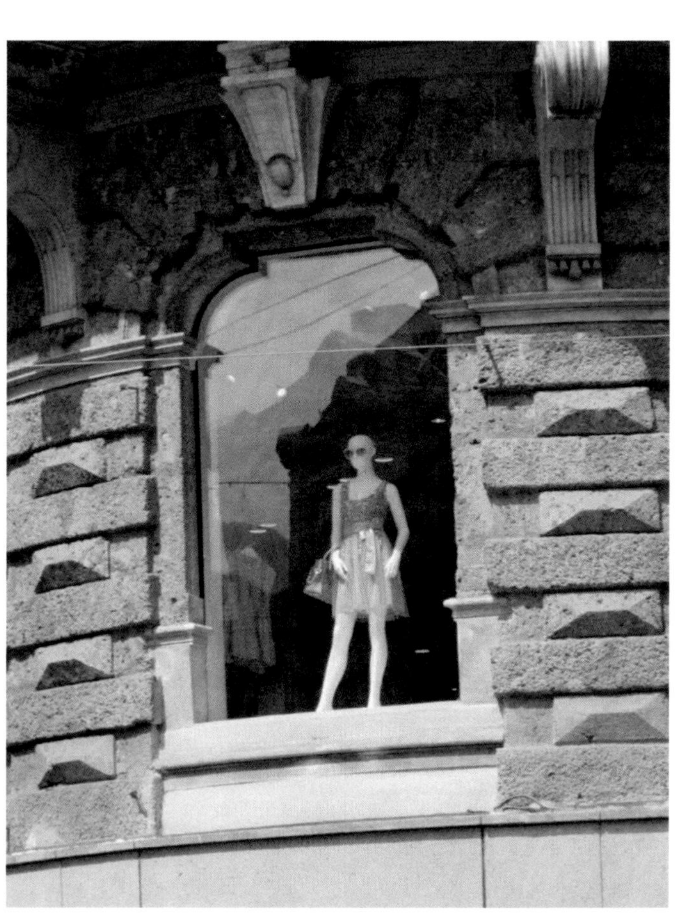

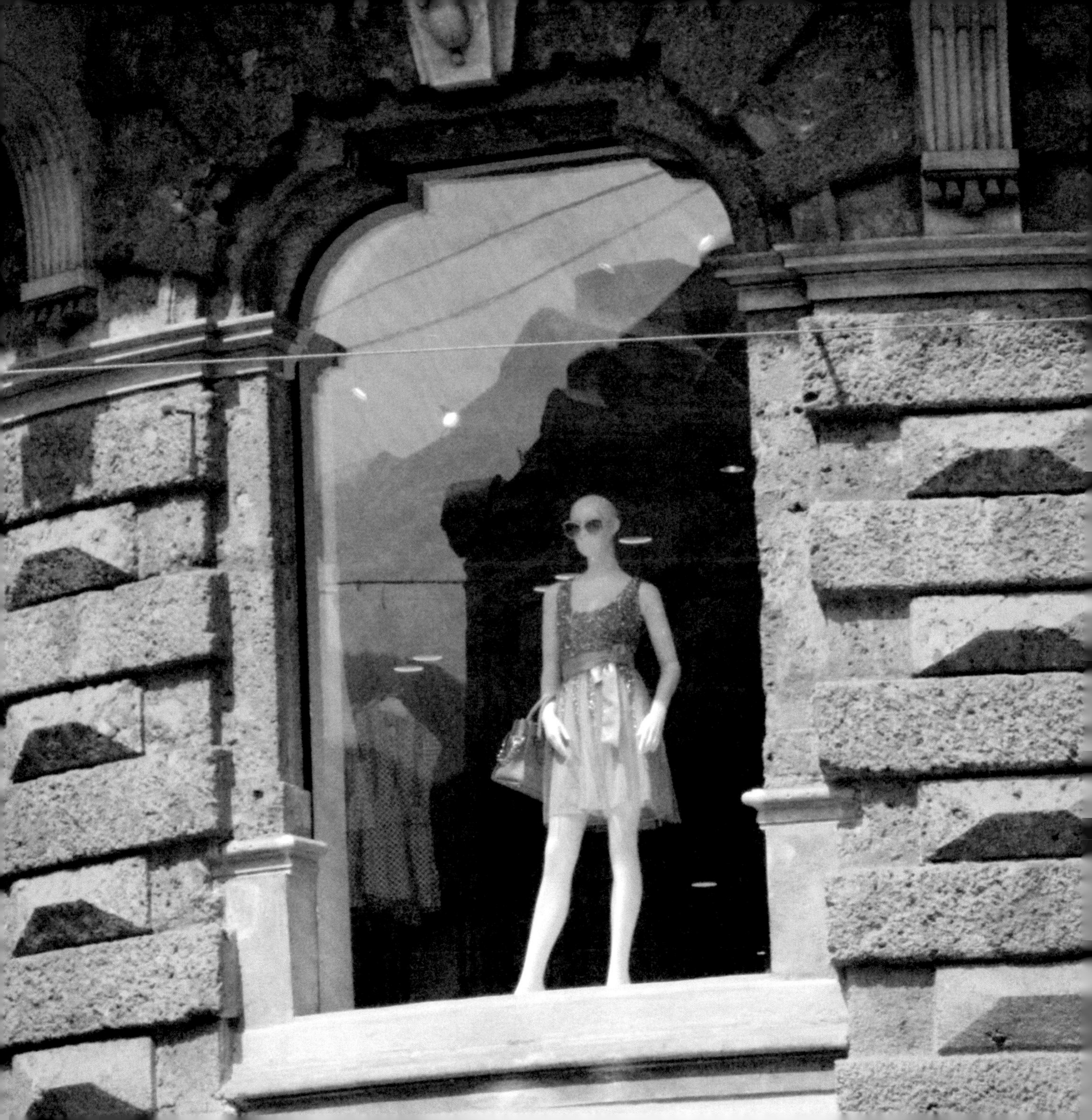

IMAGES OF THE CITY

Photo no. 38: "From above no. 2"

by Veronika Bernard

Istanbul, 2012

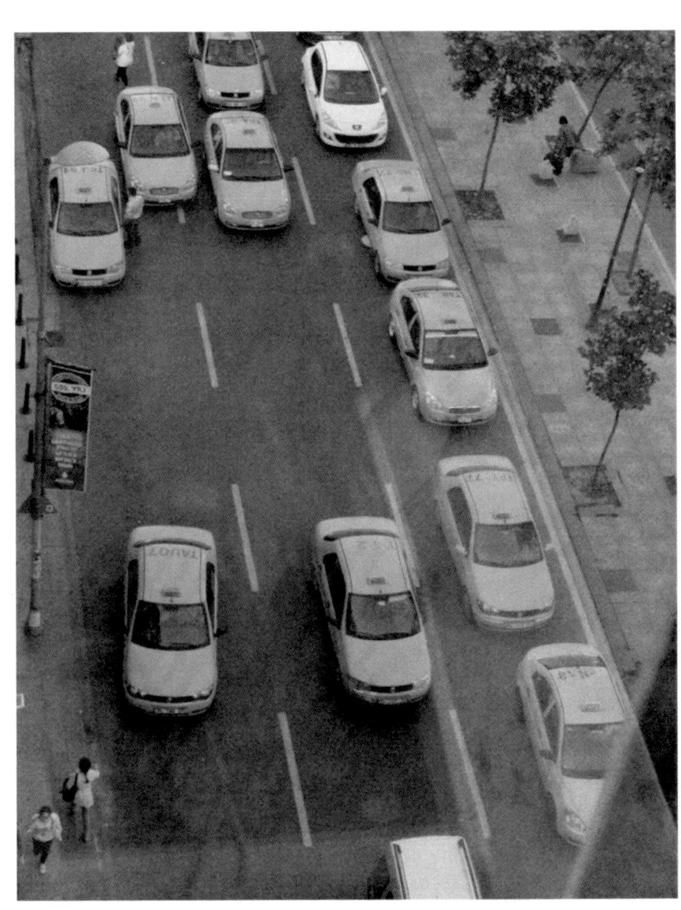

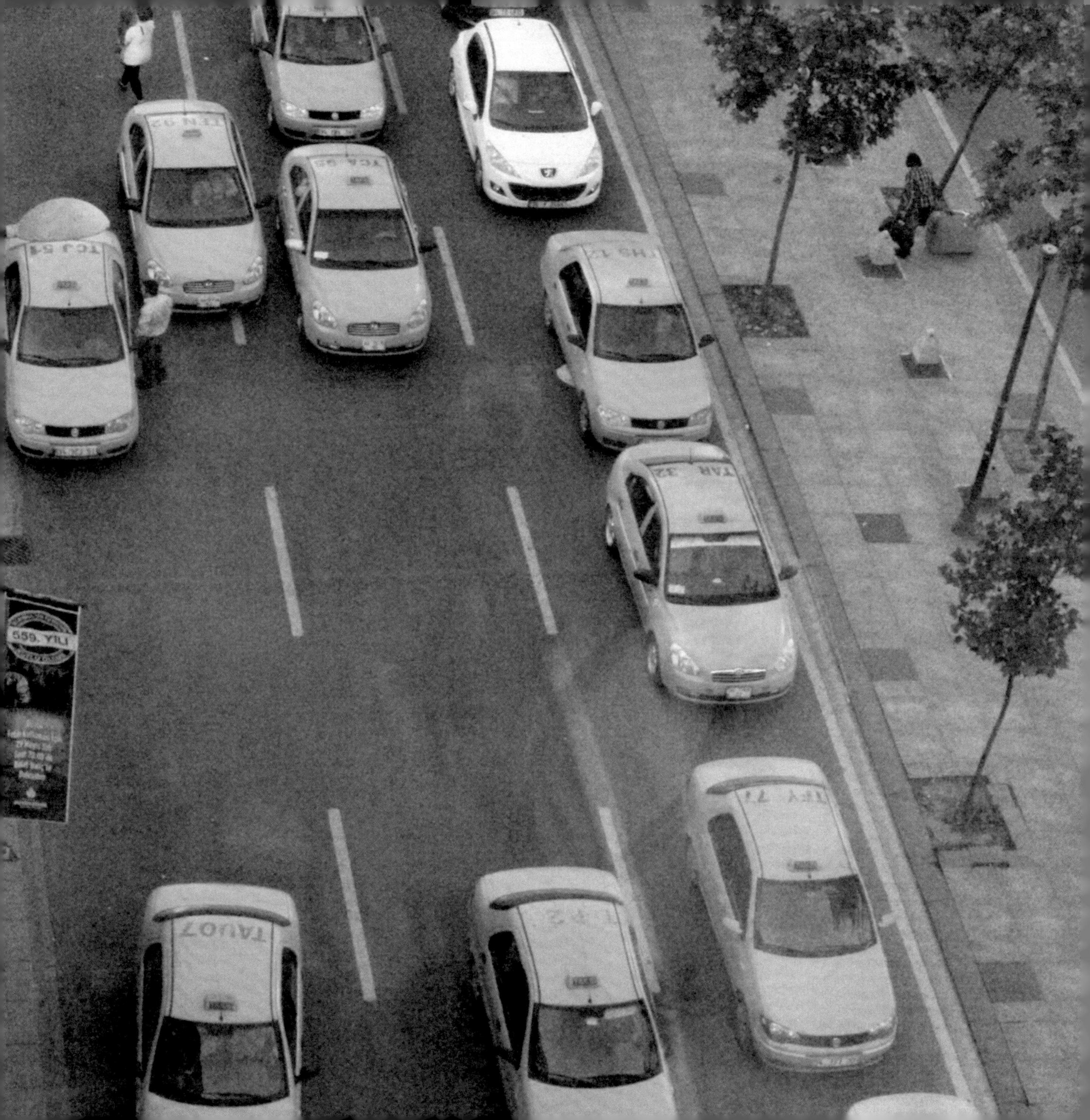
559. YILI

IMAGES OF THE CITY

Photo no. 39: “Visual Deception no. 1”

by Veronika Bernard

Istanbul, 2013

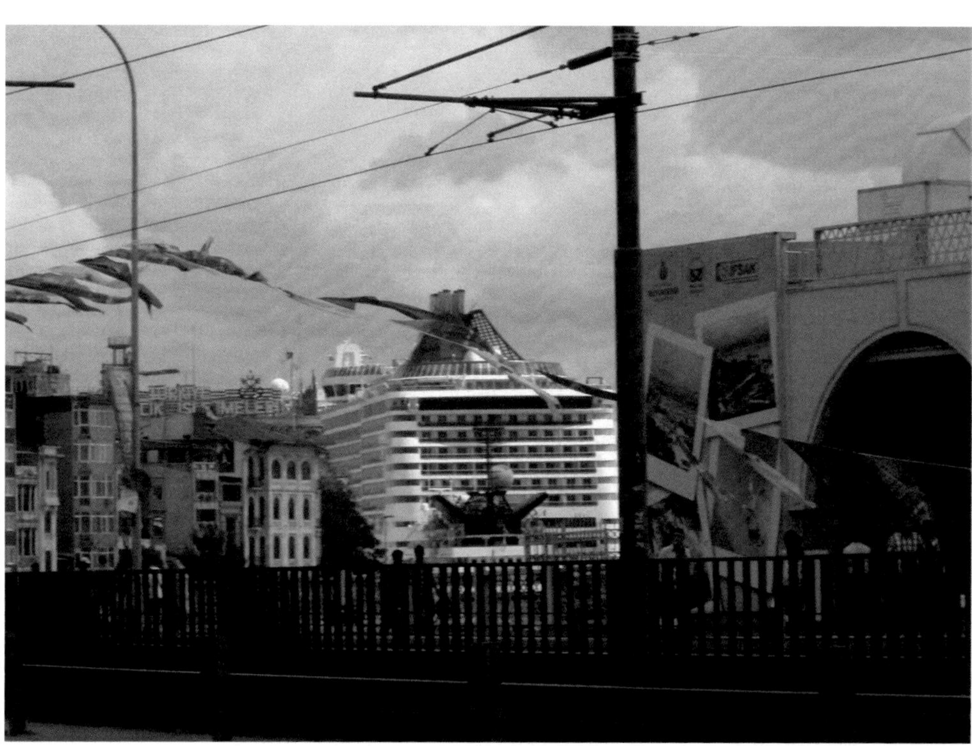

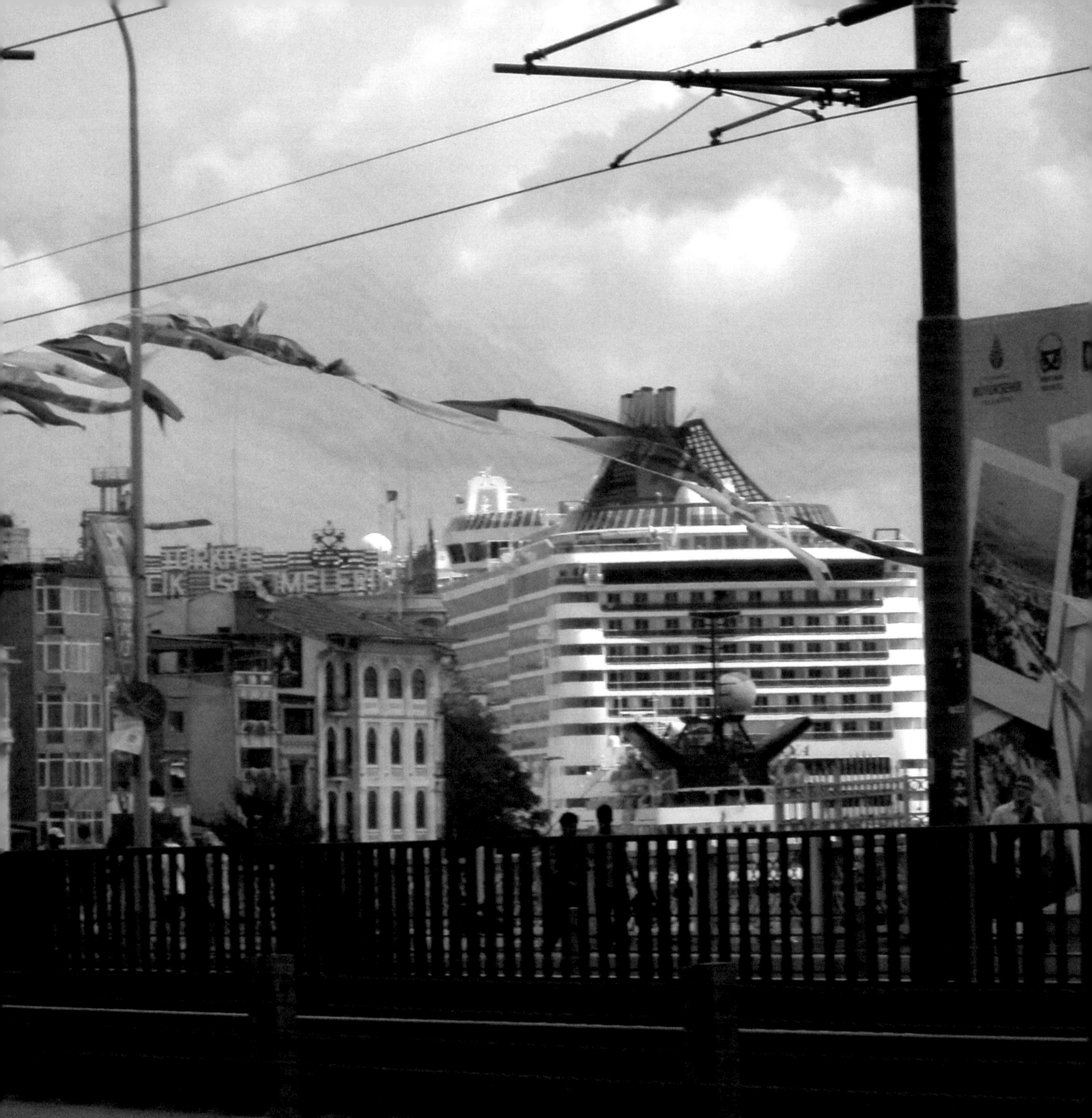

IMAGES OF THE CITY

Photo no. 40: "Nosey Vehicle"

by Veronika Bernard

Kufstein, 2013

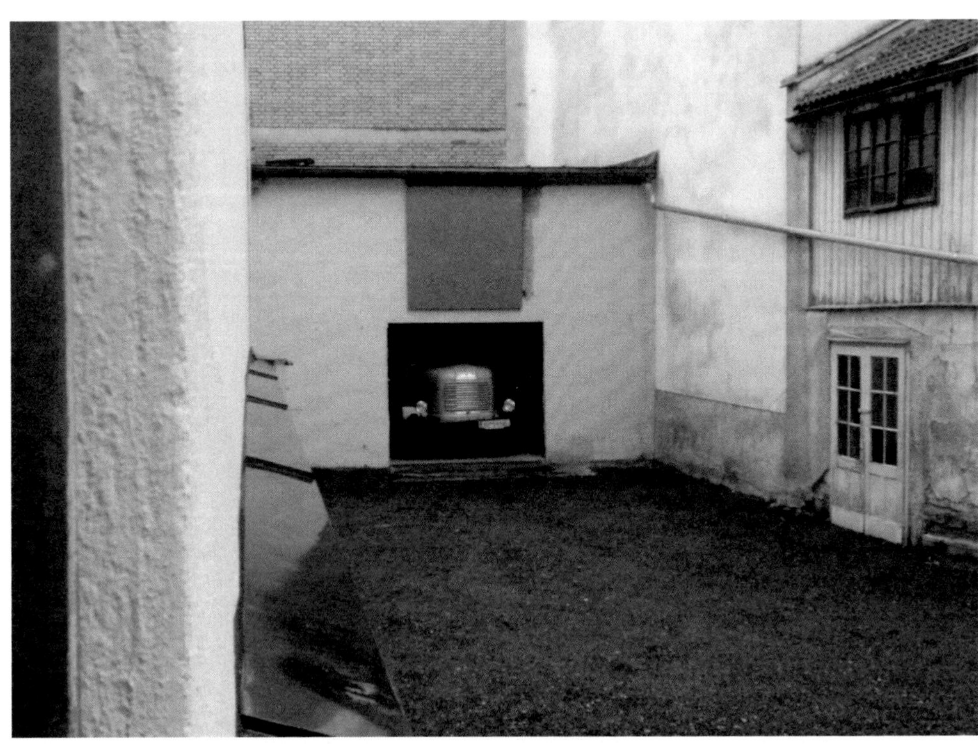

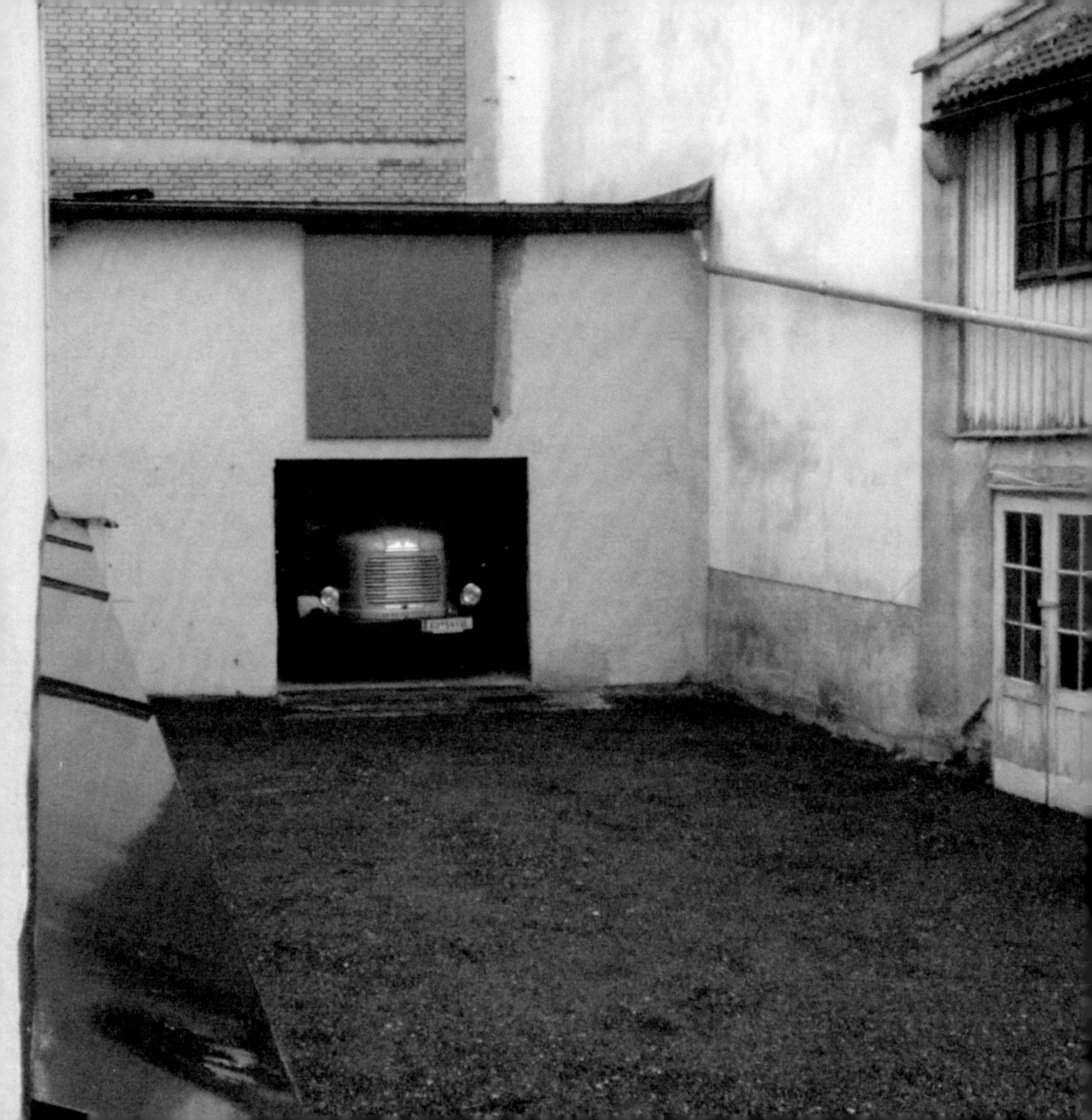

Urban Life & Arts

Urbanes Leben - Urbane Kunst

IMAGES OF THE CITY

Photo no. 41: "Fish Love"

by Veronika Bernard

Cologne (Cologne Lovelocks), 2011

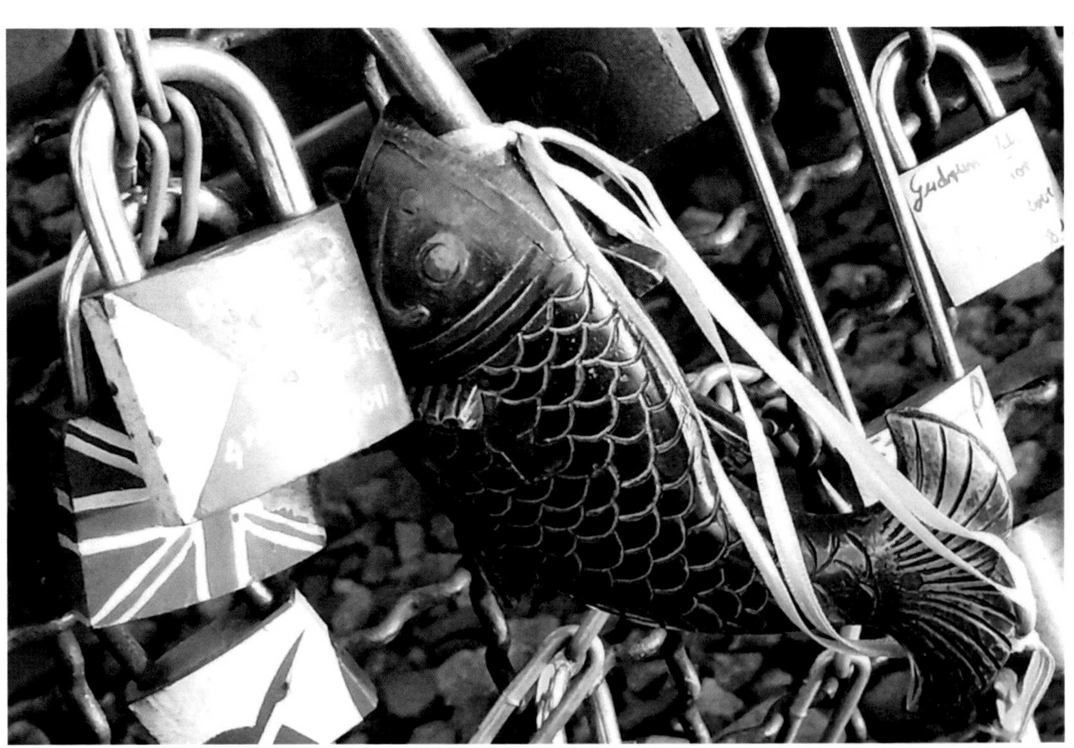

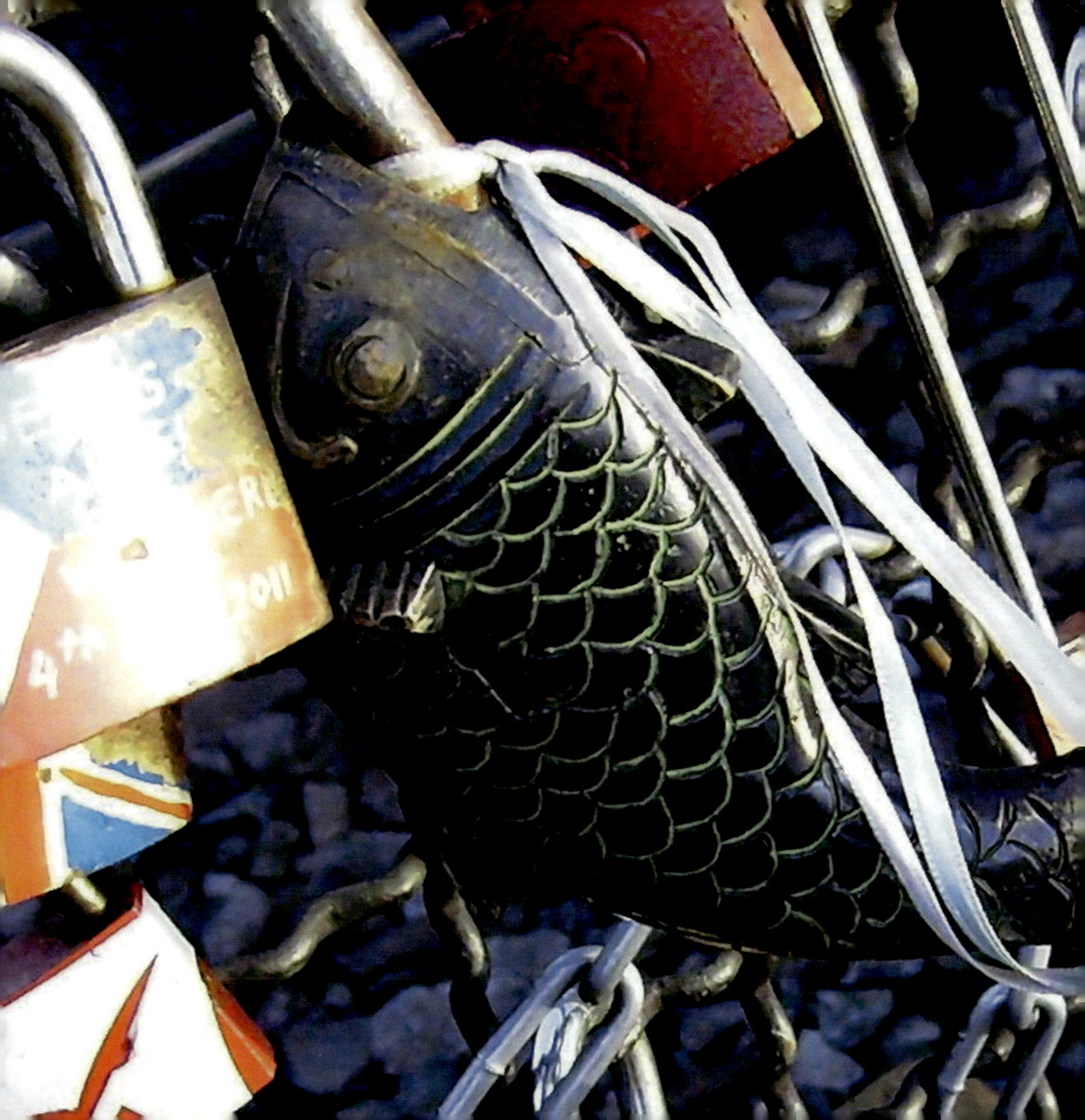

IMAGES OF THE CITY

Photo no. 42: "Visual Fakes"

by Veronika Bernard

Basel, 2012

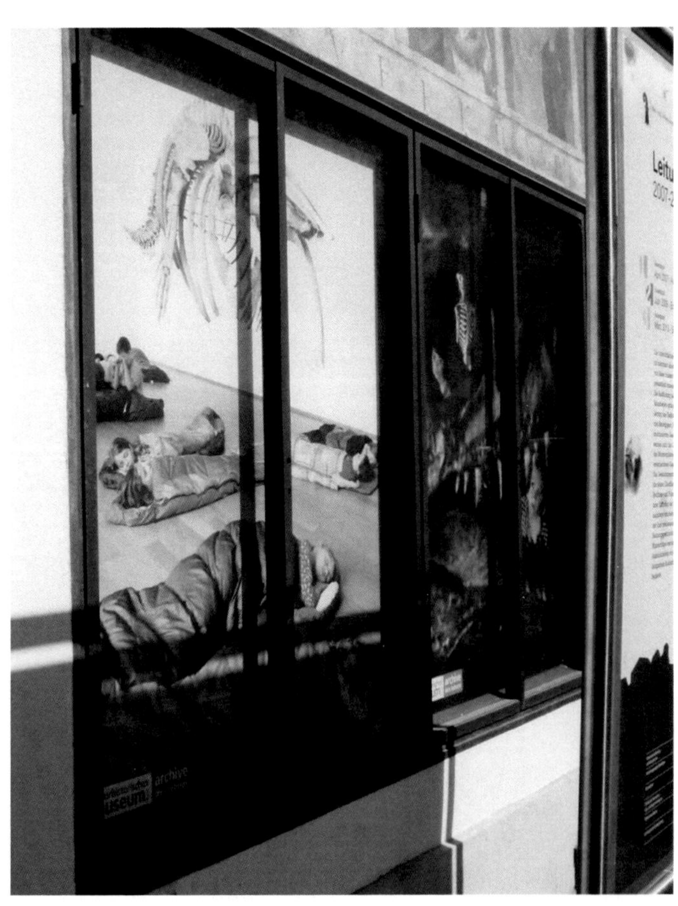

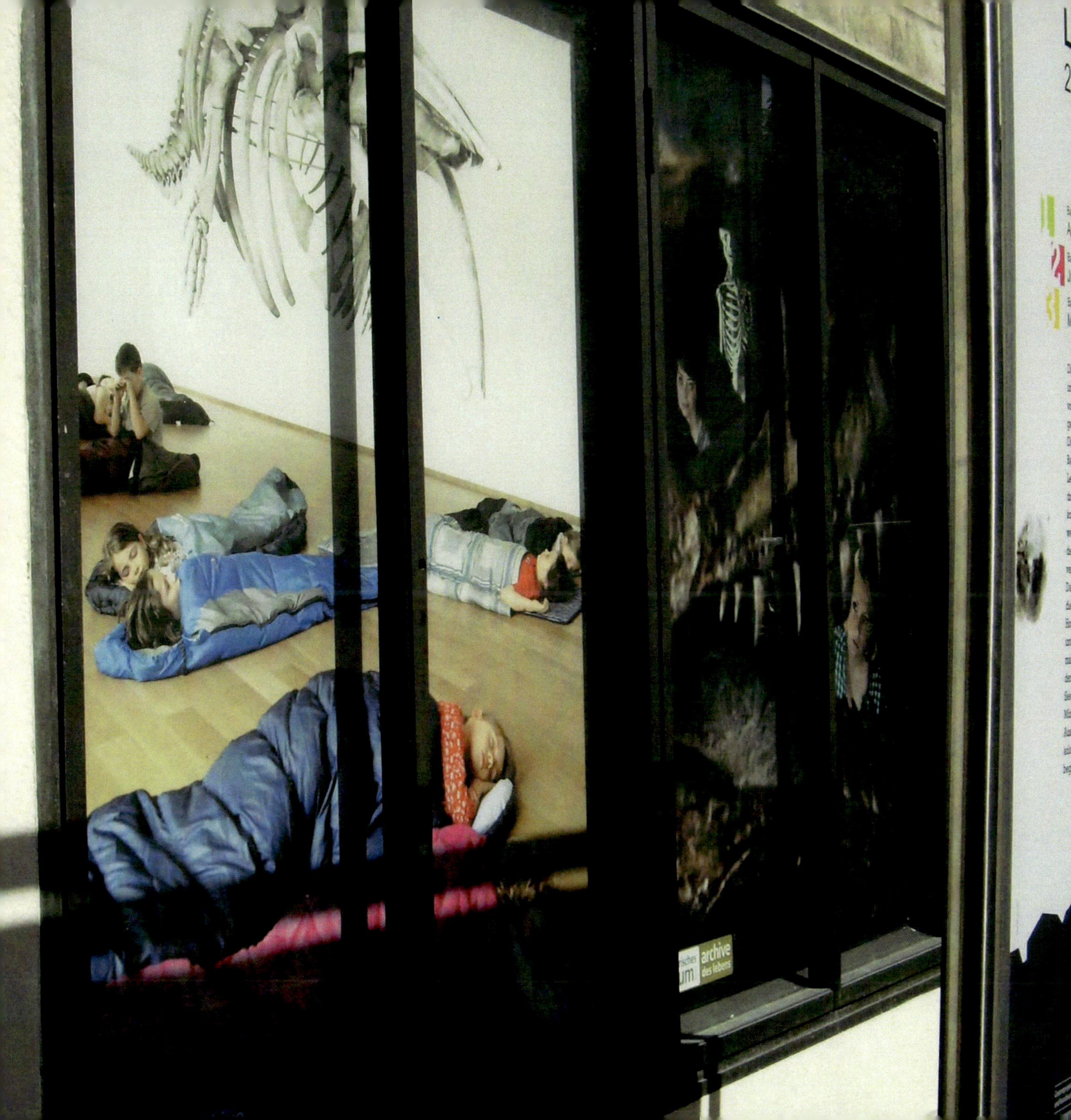
archive
des lebens

IMAGES OF THE CITY

Photo no. 43: "Eloquent Walls no. 1"

by Veronika Bernard

Arles, 2011

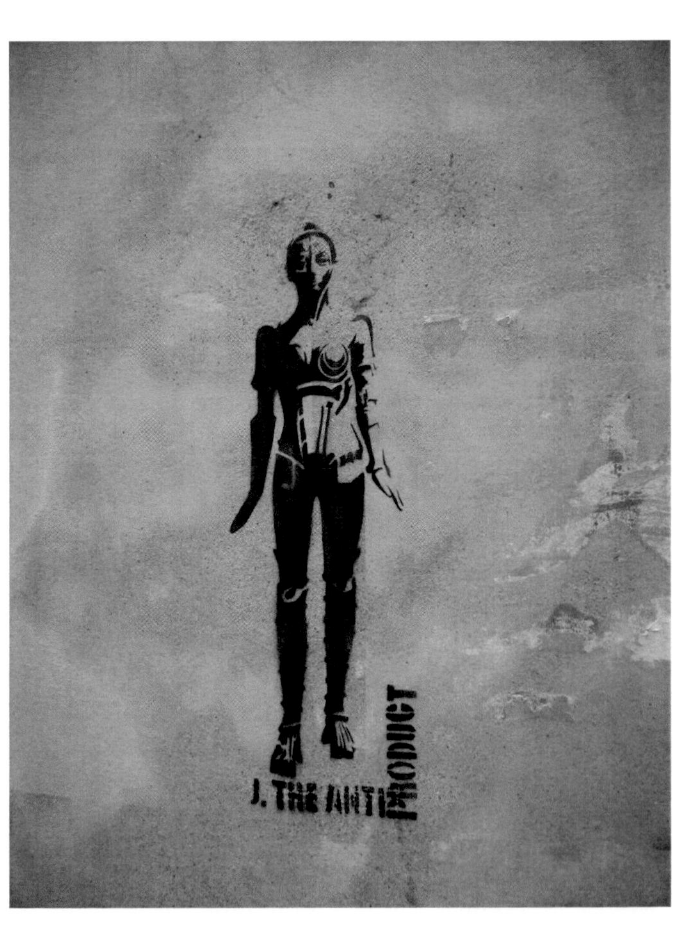

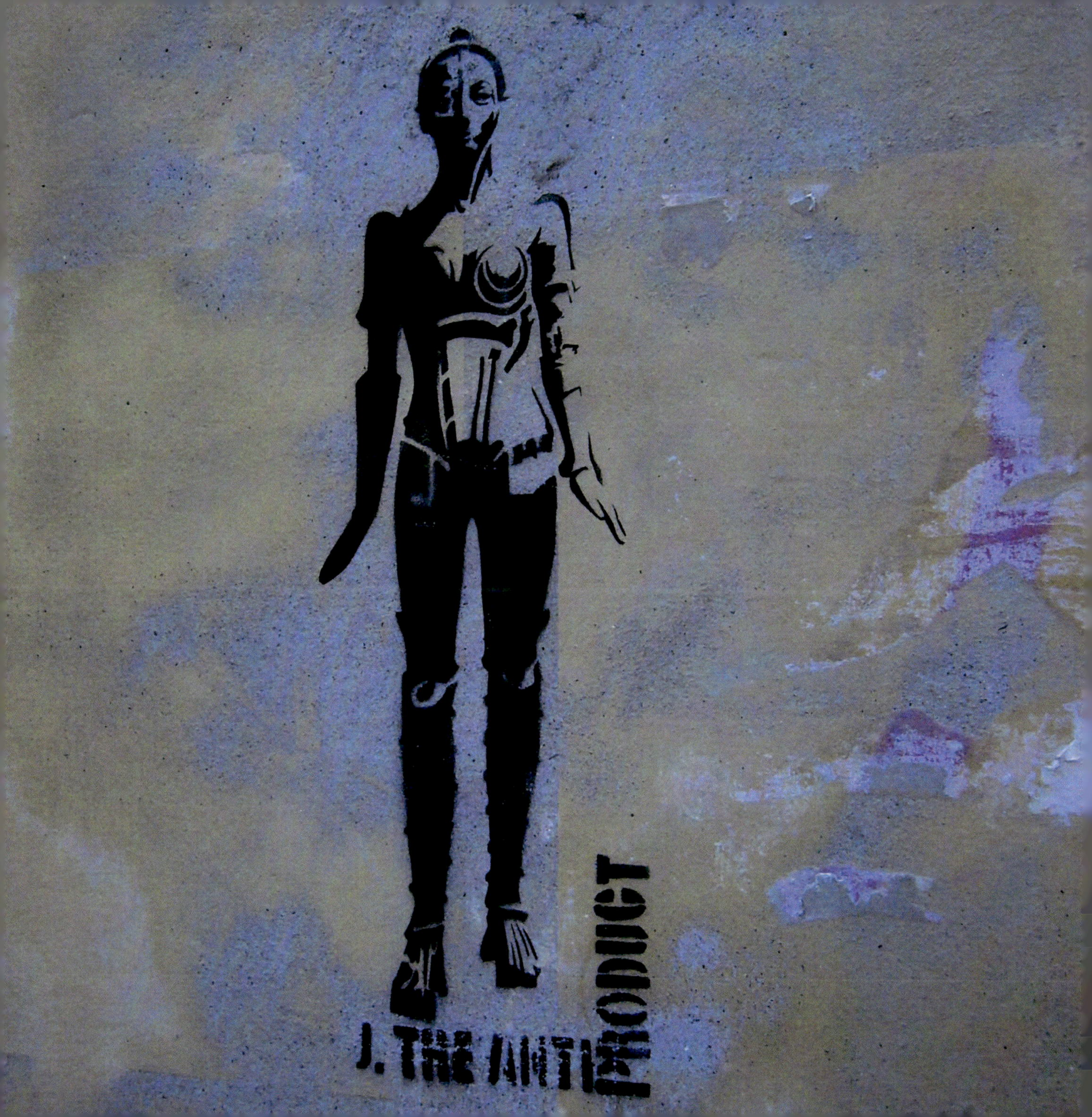
J. THE ANTI
PRODUCT

IMAGES OF THE CITY

Photo no. 44: "Eloquent Walls no. 2"

by Veronika Bernard

Arles, 2011

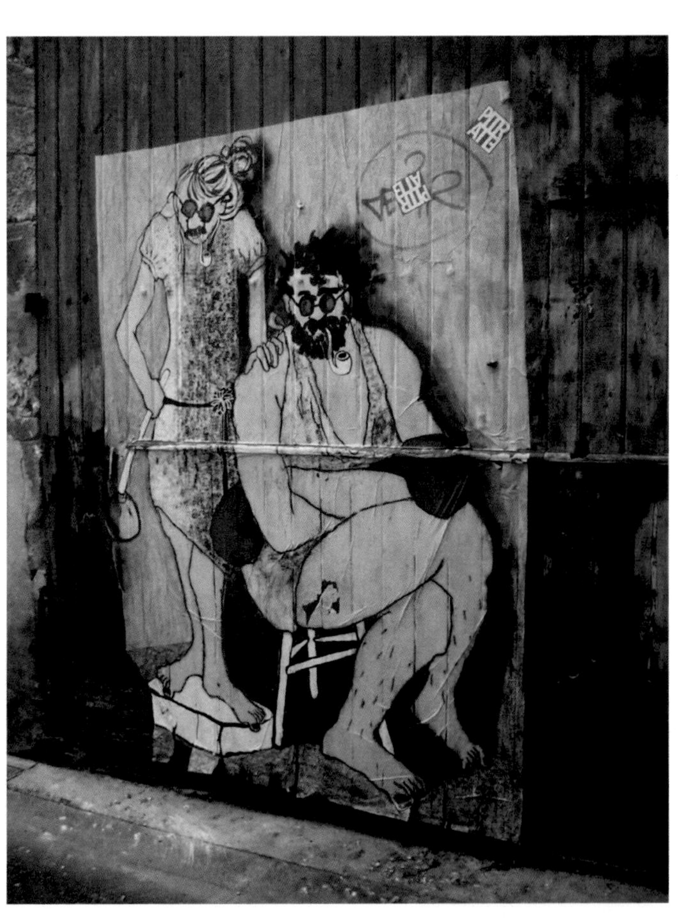

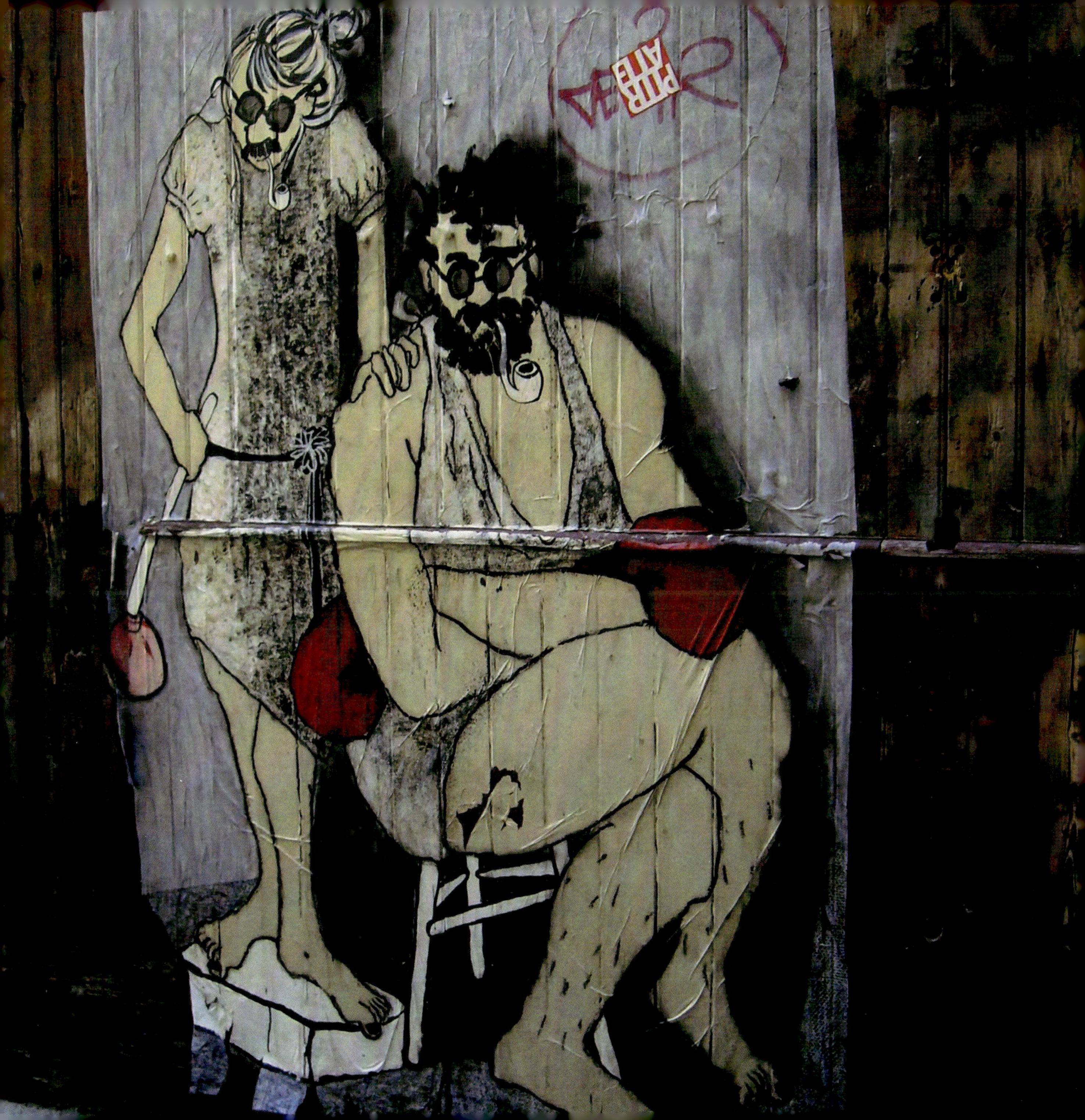

IMAGES OF THE CITY

Photo no. 45: "Graffiti Comics"

by Veronika Bernard

Bratislava, 2013

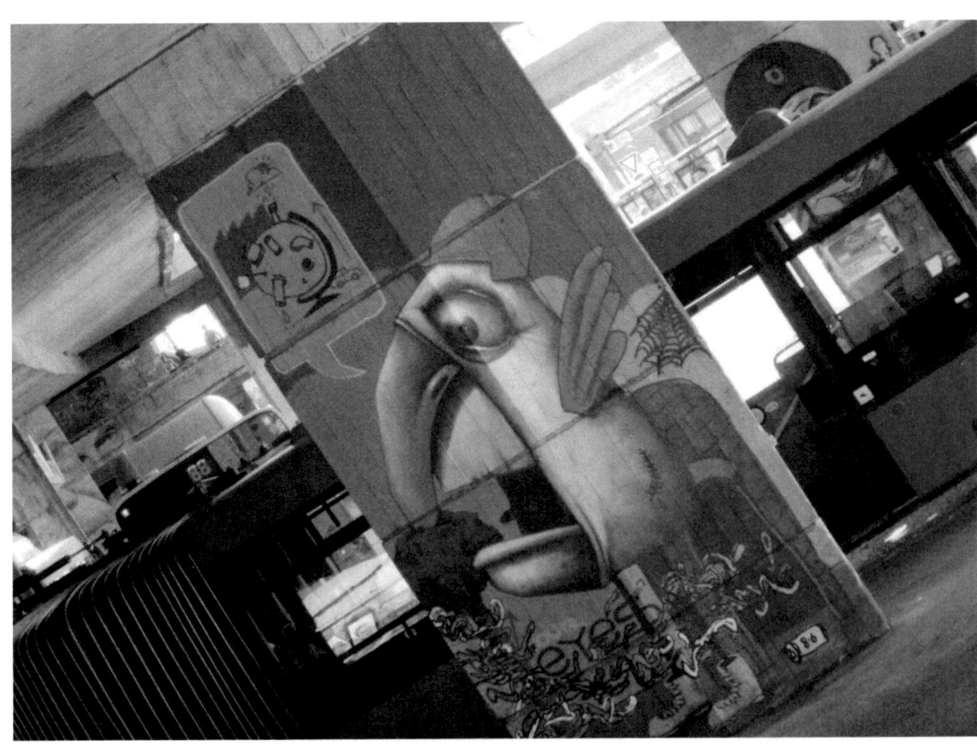

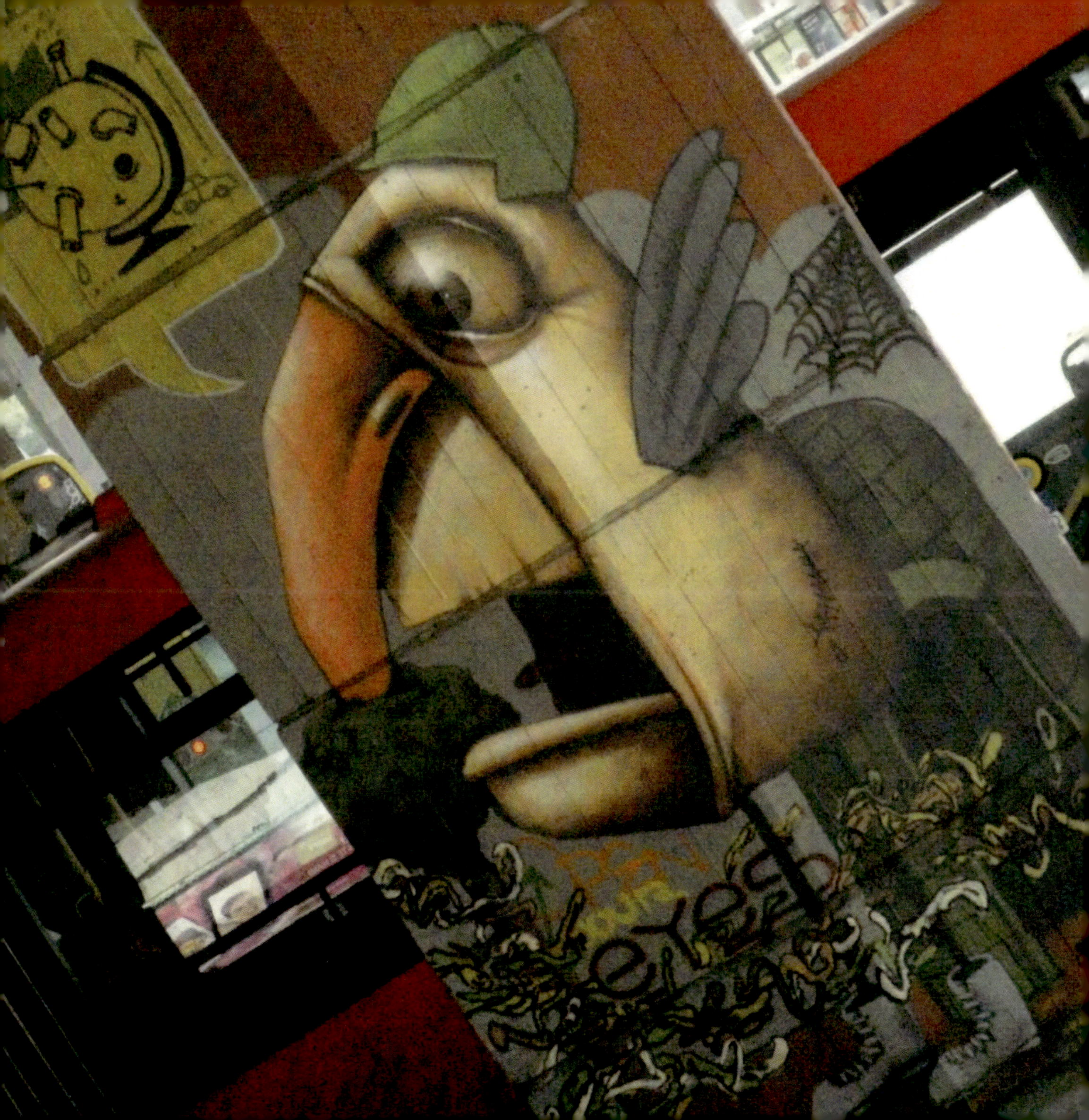

IMAGES OF THE CITY

Photo no. 46: "Eloquent Walls no. 3"

by Veronika Bernard

Arles, 2011

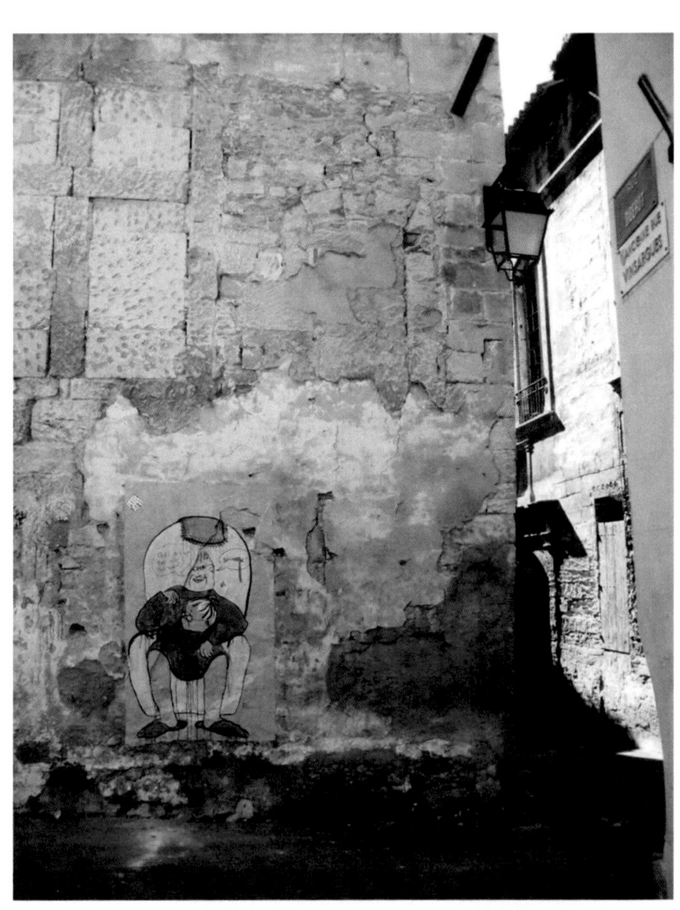

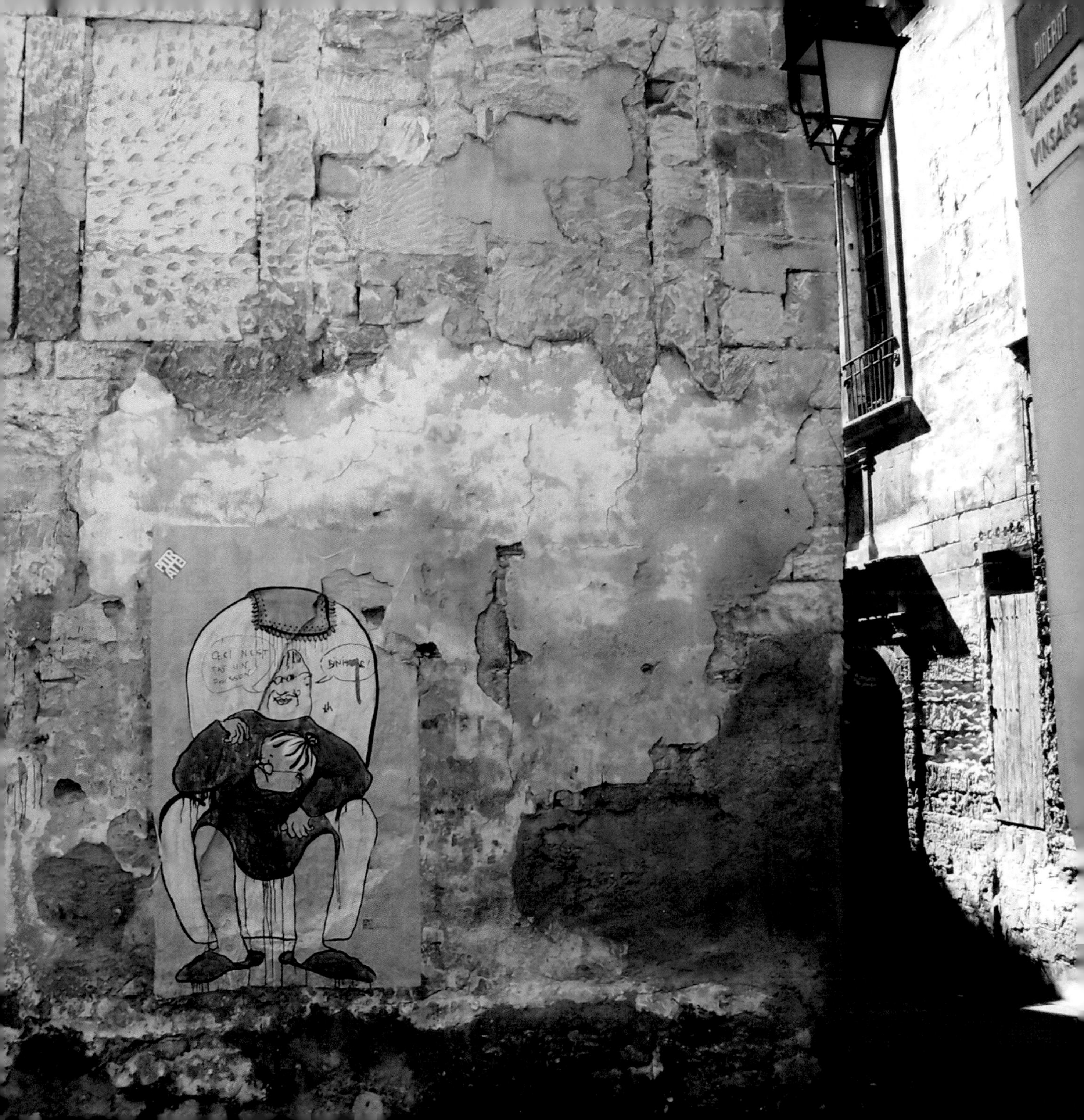
CECI N'EST PAS UN POISSON
DIDEROT
ANCIENNE

IMAGES OF THE CITY

Photo no. 47: "Of Cats & Dogs"

by Veronika Bernard

Innsbruck, 2012

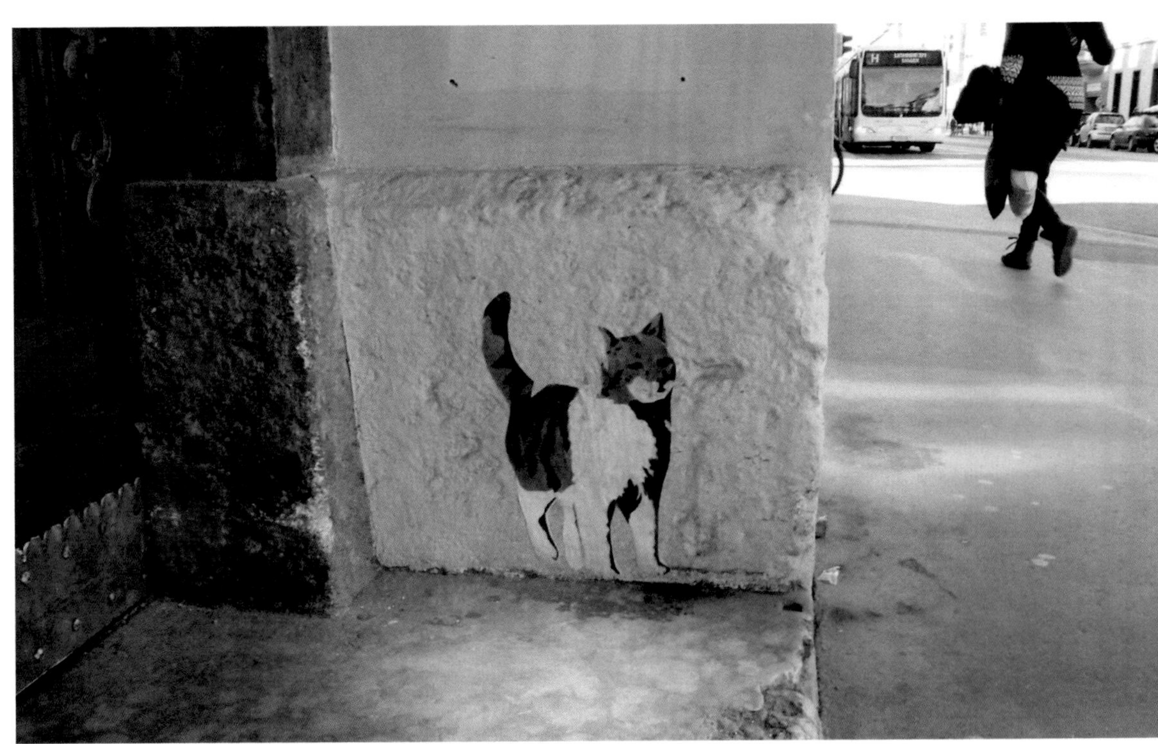

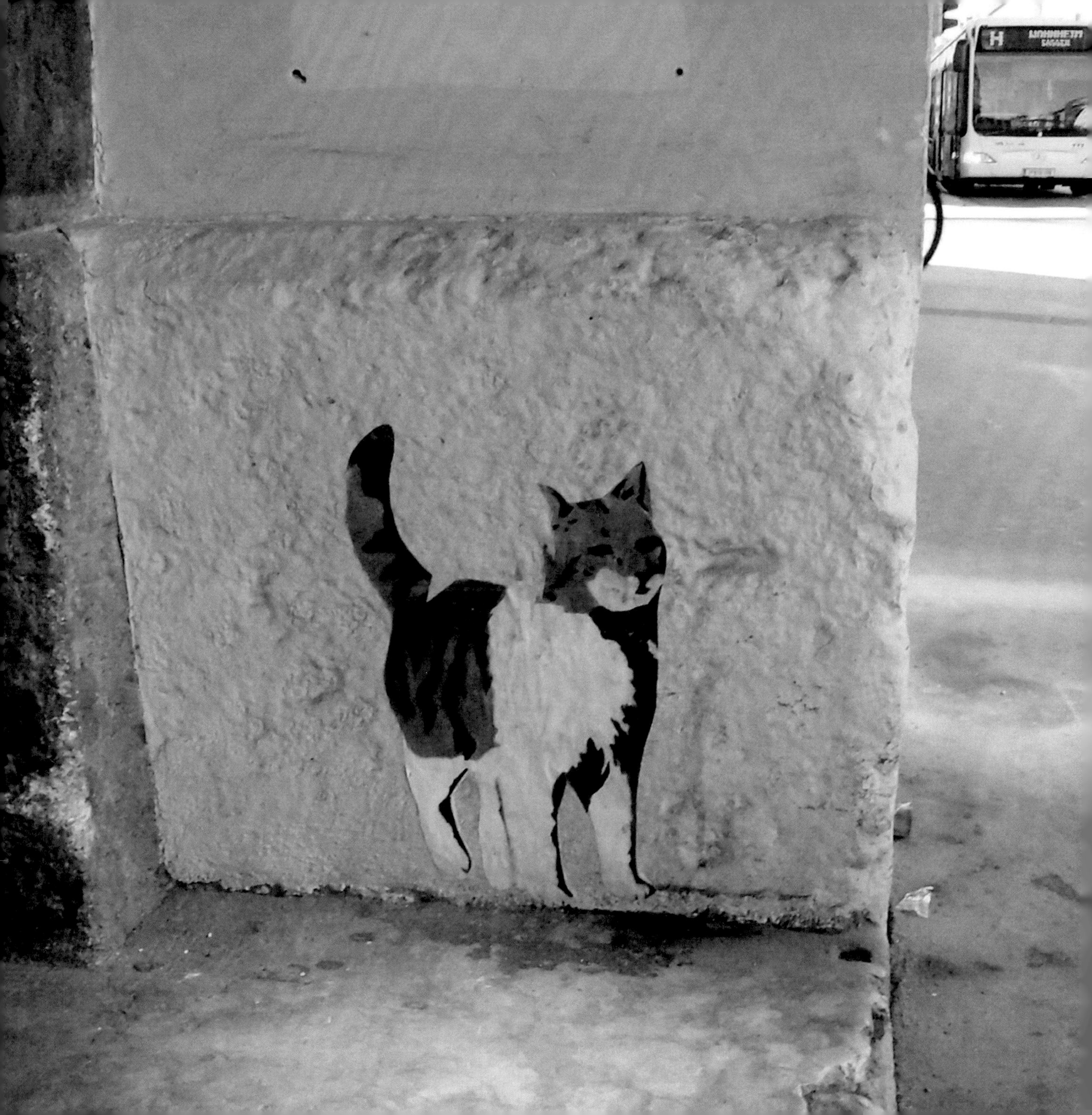

IMAGES OF THE CITY

Photo no. 48: "Made for Giants"

by Veronika Bernard

Cologne (Rheinauhafen), 2013

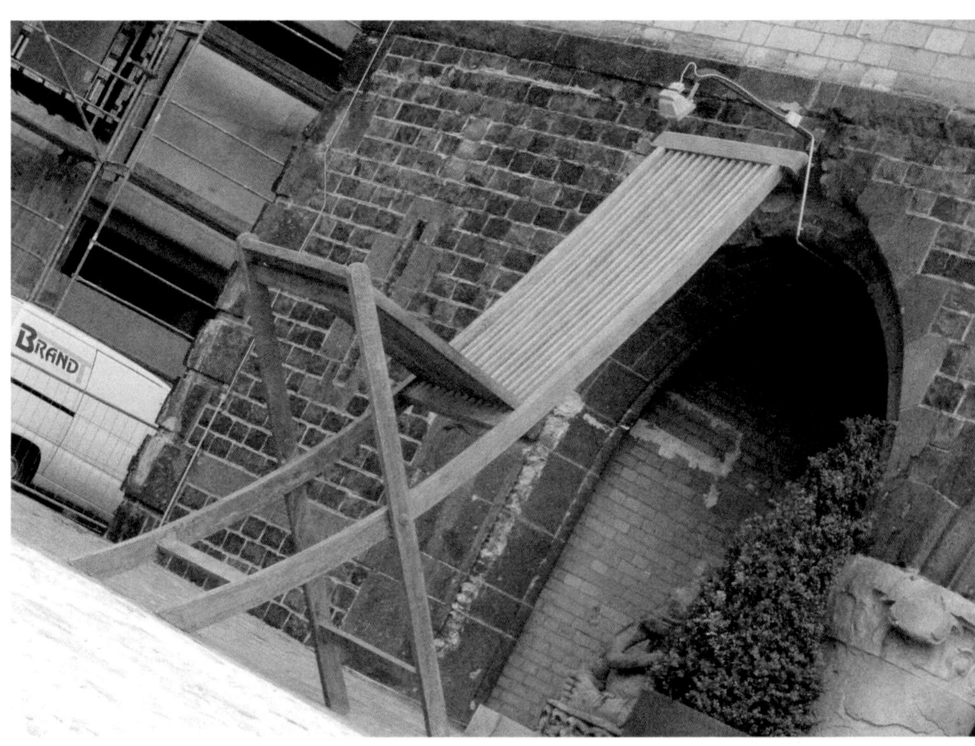

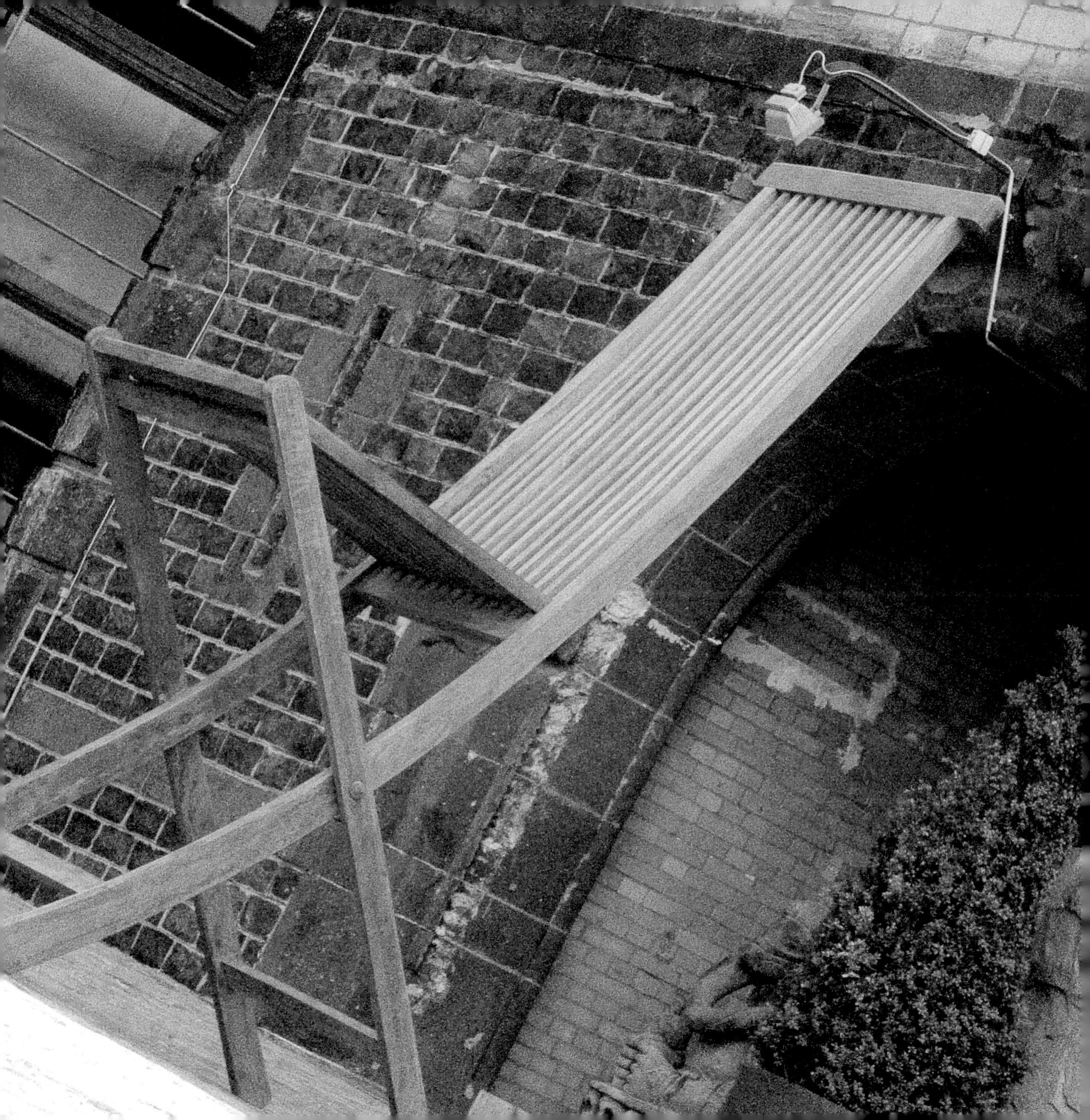

IMAGES OF THE CITY

Photo no. 49: "1984"

by Veronika Bernard

Bratislava, 2013

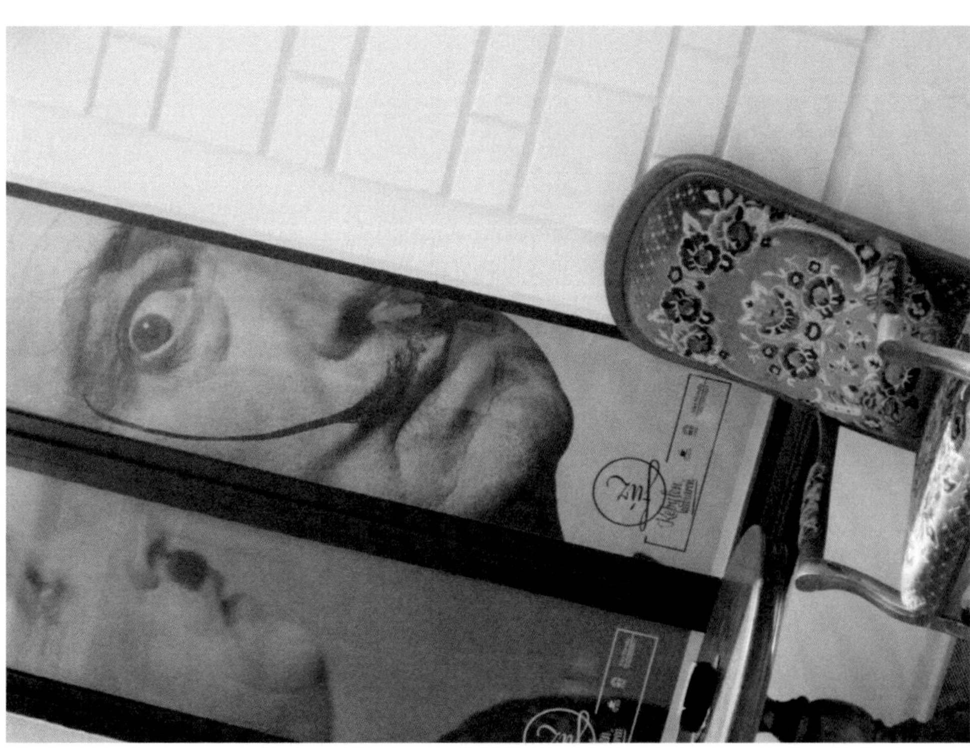

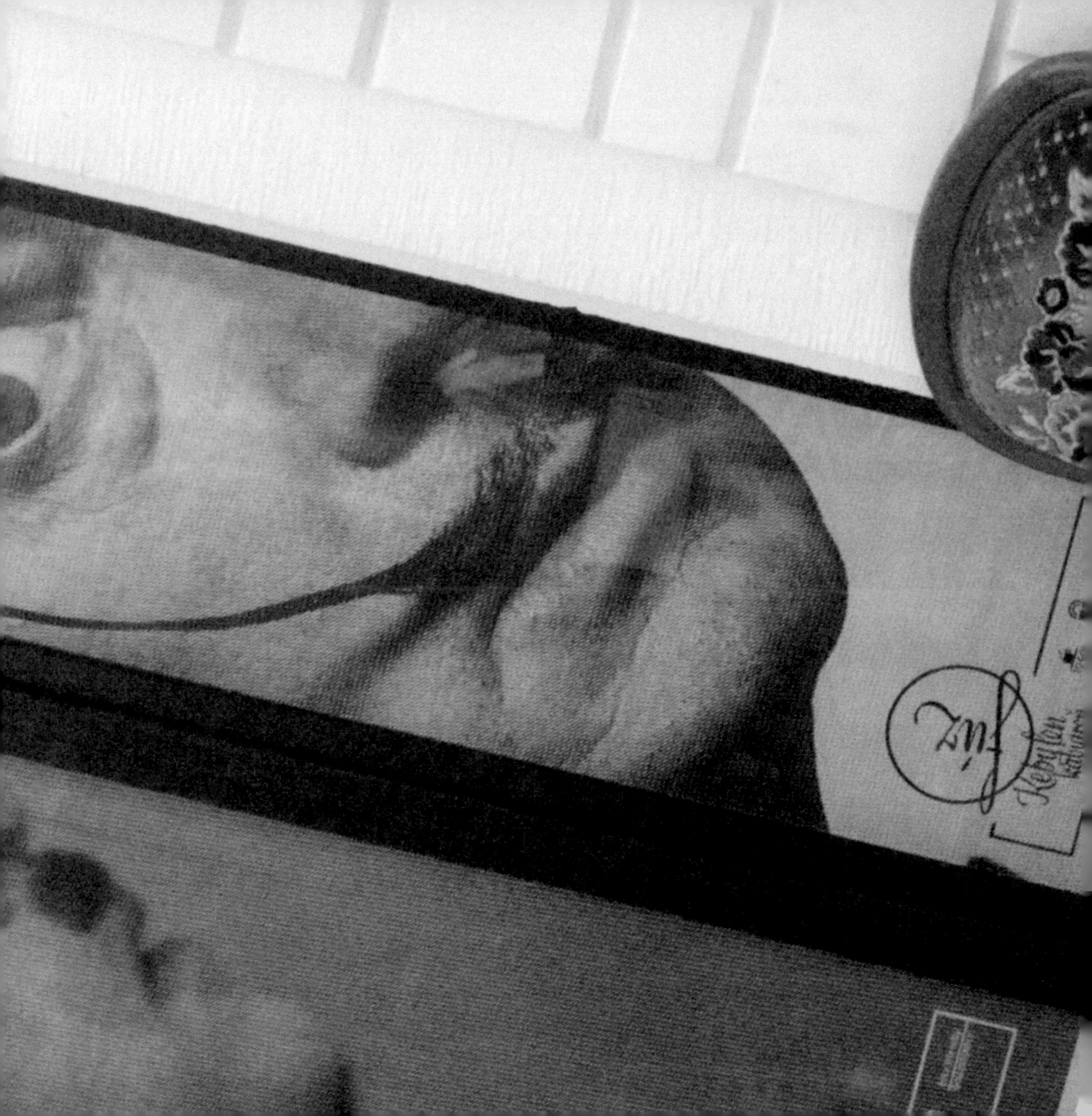

IMAGES OF THE CITY

Photo no. 50: "Love Bites"

by Veronika Bernard

Cologne (Cologne Lovelocks), 2013

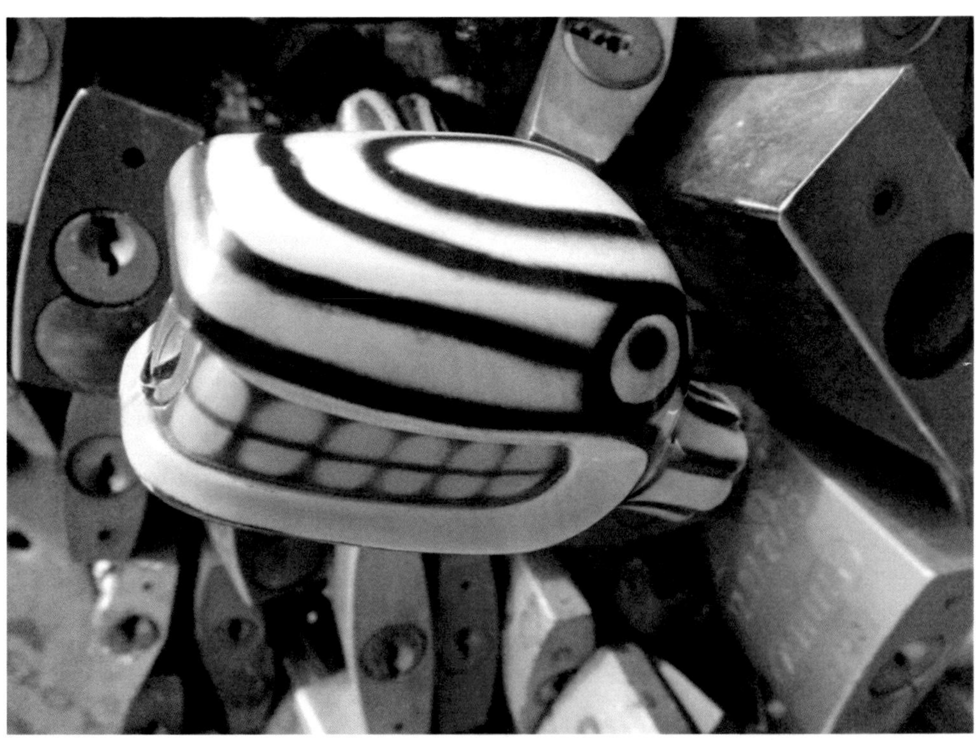

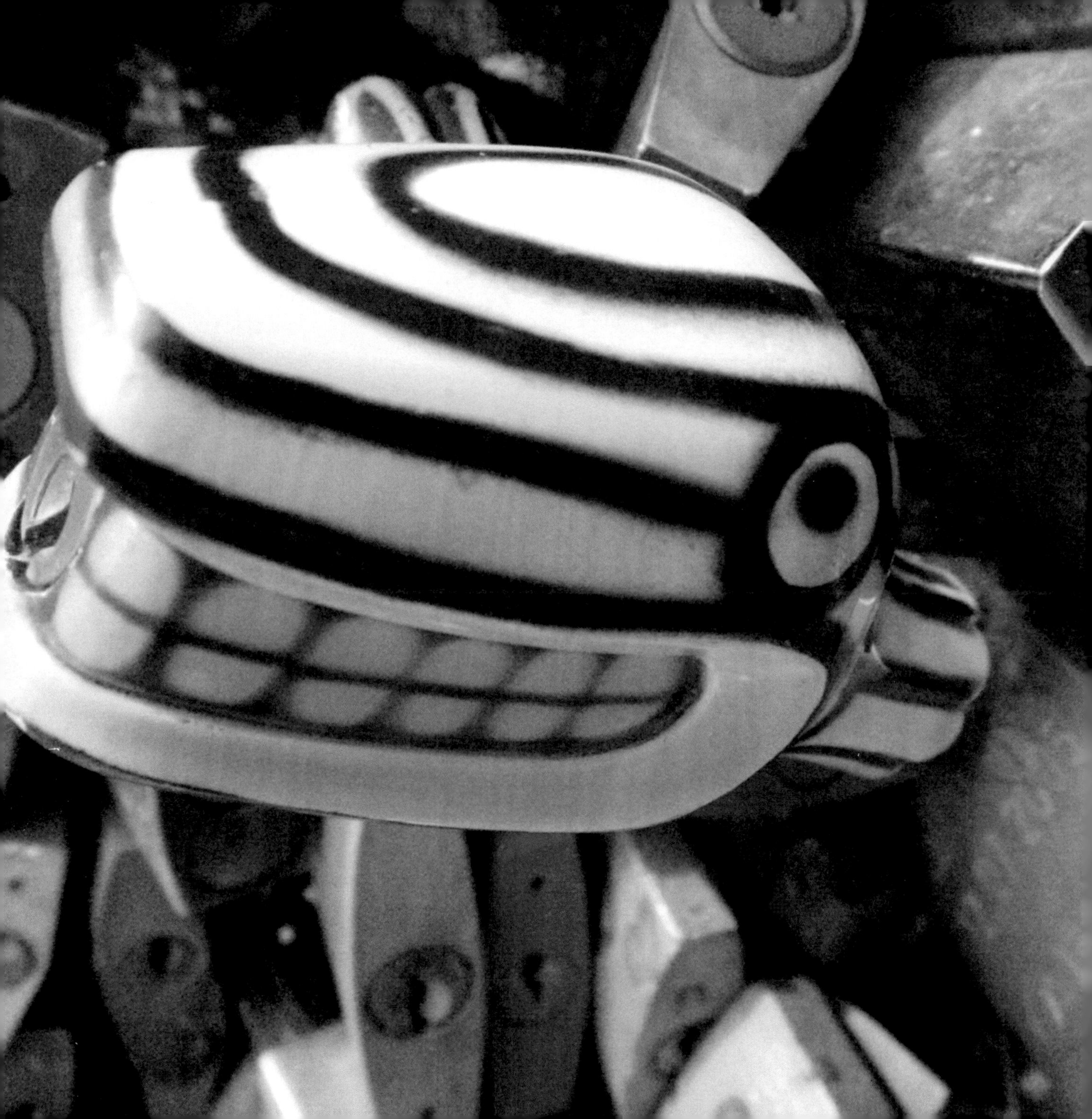

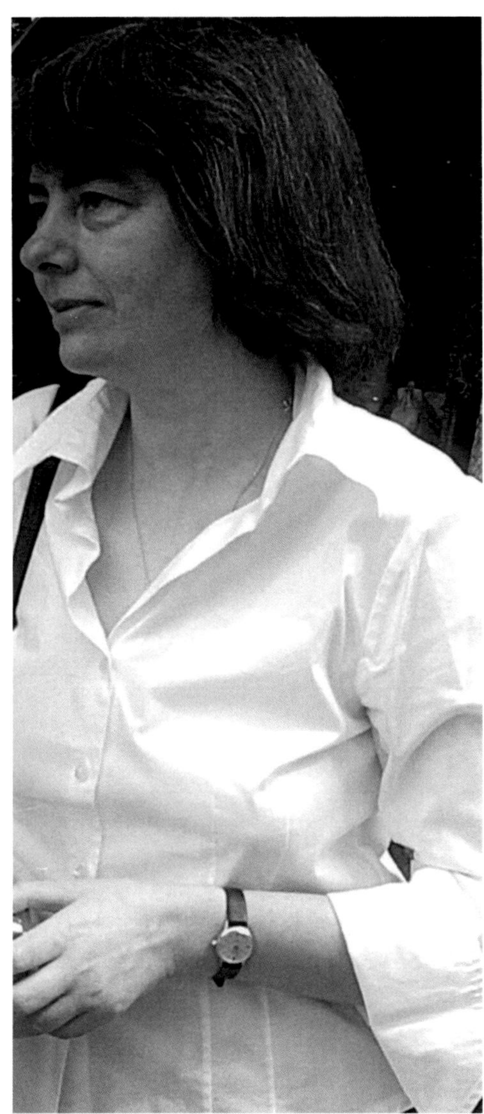

Photo © by Serhan Oksay (2009)

Veronika Bernard

Veronika Bernard is an Associate Professor (Privatdozentin) with the Department of German Language and Literature at the University of Innsbruck (Austria) and an artist whose works are based on photography.
Find her *ORNAMENTAL ABSTRACTIONS* works gallery and her *ORNAMENTAL ABSTRACTIONS Design Line* on her homepage http://ornamental-abstractions.weebly.com.
Follow her projects on her blogs:
http://ornamentalabstractions.over-blog.com
http://snapshots-1.over-blog.com
http://images-1.over-blog.org.

Veronika Bernard ist Privatdozentin für deutsche Literatur am Institut für Germanistik der Universität Innsbruck (Österreich) und mit Fotografie arbeitende Künstlerin.
Ihre *ORNAMENTAL ABSTRACTIONS* Galerie und *ORNAMENTAL ABSTRACTIONS Design Line* Kreationen finden Sie auf ihrer Homepage http://ornamental-abstractions-de.weebly.com (deutsch).
Ihren Projekten können Sie auf den jeweiligen Blogs folgen:
http://ornamentalabstractions.over-blog.com,
http://snapshots-1.over-blog.com
http://images-1.over-blog.org.

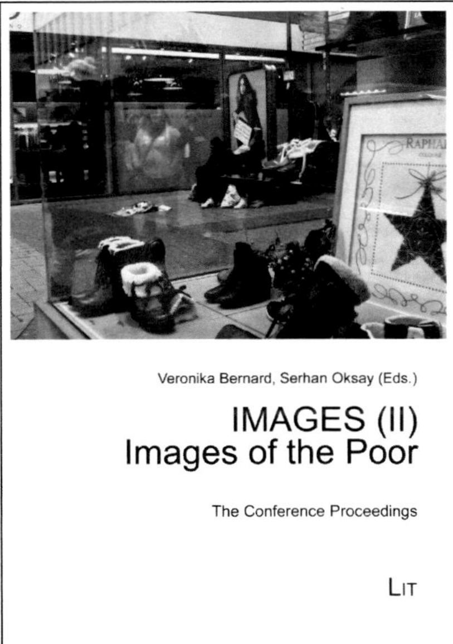

Veronika Bernard; Serhan Oksay (Eds.)
IMAGES (II) – Images of the Poor
The Conference Proceedings

IMAGES (II) – Images of the Poor offers readers a cross-section of current research on the perception of poverty and on contemporary and historical representations of poverty coming from a variety of fields in people's daily lives. The fact that the international group of contributors to this volume is writing from very different cultural, ideological, scientific and academic perspectives and backgrounds is adding even more to the diversity of thought and ideas documented. The arguments presented in the articles aim at raising the social awareness needed to break the vicious circle of poverty.

Ethnologie, vol. 52, 2013, ca. 272 pp., ca. 29,90 €, br.,
ISBN-CH 978-3-643-90363-1

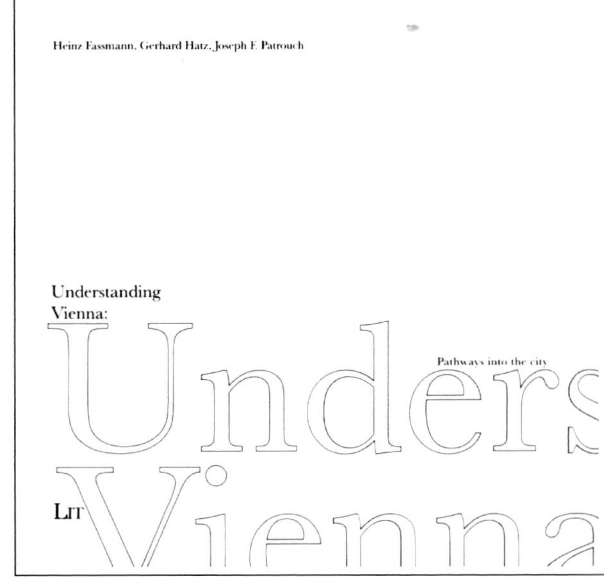

Heinz Faßmann; Gerhard Hatz; Joseph F. Patrouch
Understanding Vienna
Path Ways to the City

What is it that makes Vienna so fascinating for visitors and inhabitants alike?

The reader ist invited to join 12 excursions, each dedicated to specific topics, and personally discover aspects of Vienna by following each path. The walks illustrate the historical and physical development of the old city center, they lead to zones of gentle urban renewal and public housing, and point out Vienna's multiethnic past as well as its culturally diverse present. By following the suggested pathways, shopping may become a learning experience and the reader gets the chance to explore the endless cycle of performances and festivals promoting the image of Vienna.

Viennensia, vol. 1, 2007, 304 pp., 19,90 €, br., ISBN-DE 978-3-8258-0093-8,
ISBN-AT 978-3-7000-0659-6

LIT Verlag Berlin – Münster – Wien – Zürich – London
Auslieferung Deutschland / Österreich / Schweiz: siehe Impressumsseite